MATH

Grade 1

Thomas J. Richards
Mathematics Teacher
Lamar Junior-Senior High School
Lamar, Missouri

Marjorie Diggs Freeman
Basic Skills Enrichment Program
Shark River Hills School
Neptune, New Jersey

 **Children's Publishing**

Columbus, Ohio

Send all inquiries to:
McGraw-Hill Children's Publishing
8787 Orion Place
Columbus, Ohio 43240-4027

ISBN 1-56189-901-1

4 5 6 7 8 9 10 VHG 07 06 05 04

The McGraw·Hill Companies

Table of Contents

SPECTRUM MATHEMATICS

For each chapter there is instructional material, written exercises, verbal problems, and a CHECKUP. There is also a 2-page CHECKUP covering the first half of the book and a 4-page FINAL CHECKUP covering the entire book.

Record of Checkup Scores

Rank	Test Pages									
	10	18	30	44	56	70	88	109–10	111–2	113–6
Excellent	12, 11	36, 35	30	30	36, 35	8, 7	25	40, 35	40, 35	80, 70
Very Good	10, 9	30, 25	25	25	30, 25	6	20	30	30	60
Good	8, 7, 6	20	20, 15	20, 15	20	5, 4	15	25, 20	25, 20	50, 40
Fair	5, 4	15, 10	10	10	15	3	10	15	15	30
Poor	3, 2, 1, 0	10, 5, 0	5, 0	5, 0	10, 5, 0	2, 1, 0	5, 0	10, 5, 0	10, 5, 0	20, 10, 0

To record the score you receive on each CHECKUP:

(1) Find the vertical scale below the page number of that CHECKUP,
(2) on that vertical scale, draw a ● at the mark which represents your score.

For example, if you score the CHECKUP on page 10 as "My score: 8," draw a ● at the 8-mark on the first vertical scale. A score of 8 would show that your rank is "Good." You can check your progress from one checkup to the next by connecting the dots with a line segment.

Lesson 1   Numbers 0 Through 3

zero	one	two	three

0	1	2	3

Ring the numeral.

0   1   ②   3

0   1   2   3

0   1   2   3

0   1   2   3

0   1   2   3

0   1   2   3

Perfect score: 6   My score: _____

Lesson 2   Numbers 4 Through 7

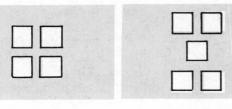
four
4

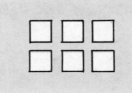
five
5

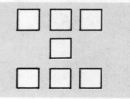
six
6

seven
7

Ring the numeral.

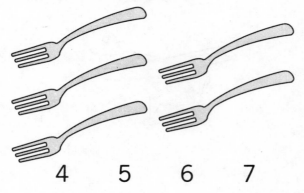

4   5   6   7

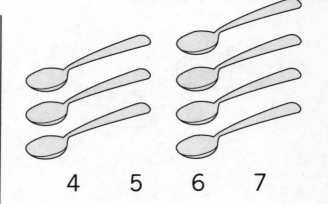

4   5   6   7

4   5   6   7

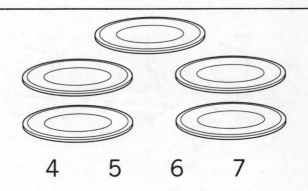

4   5   6   7

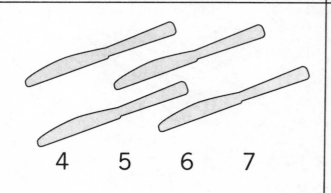

4   5   6   7

4   5   6   7

Perfect score: 6   My score: _____

Lesson 3 Numbers 8 Through 10

eight
8

nine
9

ten
10

Ring the numeral.

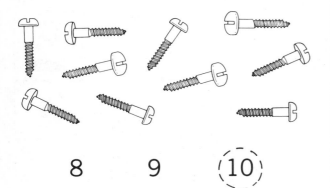

8   9   (10)

8   9   10

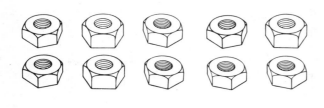

8   9   10

8   9   10

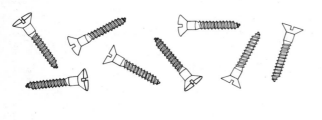

8   9   10

8   9   10

Perfect score: 6   My score: _____

3

Lesson 4　Numbers 0 Through 10

NAME _____

Read the numeral. Color that many squares.

0

1

2

3

4

5

6

7

8

9

10

Perfect score: 11　My score: _____

Lesson 5   Numbers 0 Through 10

Tell how many.

    **7**

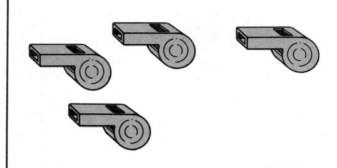   ___

     ___

   ___

      ___

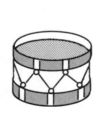 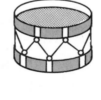   ___

   ___

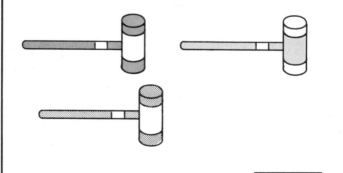   ___

Perfect score: 8   My score: _____

5

Read each name for the number.
Then draw that many ●'s.

three 3	ten 10
five 5	seven 7
two 2	eight 8
one 1	nine 9

Lesson 6   Order of Numbers

Write a numeral in each ☐ to name numbers in order.

| 1 | 2 | ☐ | ☐ | 5 |

| 6 | ☐ | ☐ | ☐ | 10 |

Count backwards. Write a numeral on each _____.

10 ____ ____ ____ 6

5 ____ ____ ____

Count forwards. Write a numeral in each ☐.

| 1 | ☐ | ☐ | ☐ | ☐ |

| 6 | ☐ | ☐ | ☐ | ☐ |

Perfect score: 20   My score: _____

Order of Numbers

Count forwards. Write the numerals in each ⬡ .
Then trace the number words on the ⎯ .

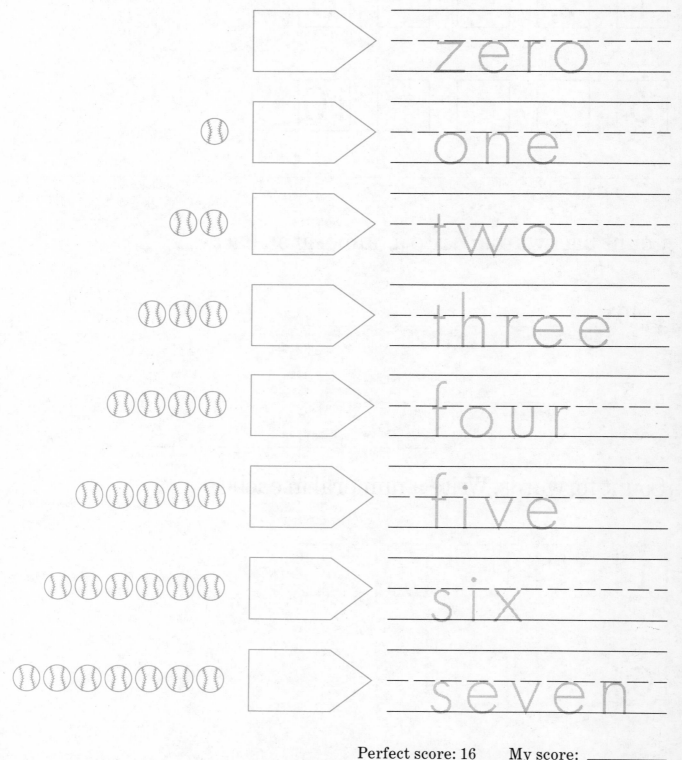

Lesson 7 Order of Numbers

Connect the dots in order.

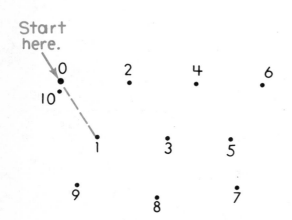

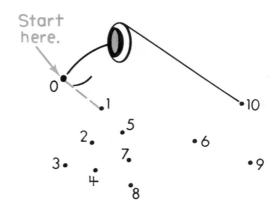

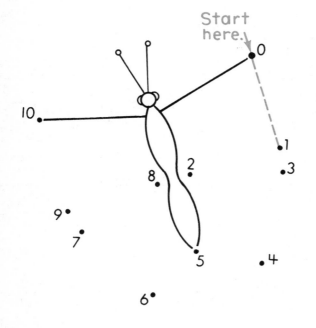

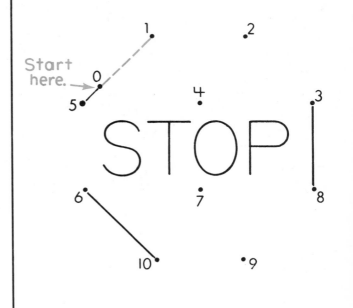

Perfect score: 4   My score: _____

9

Chapter 1 Checkup

Tell how many.

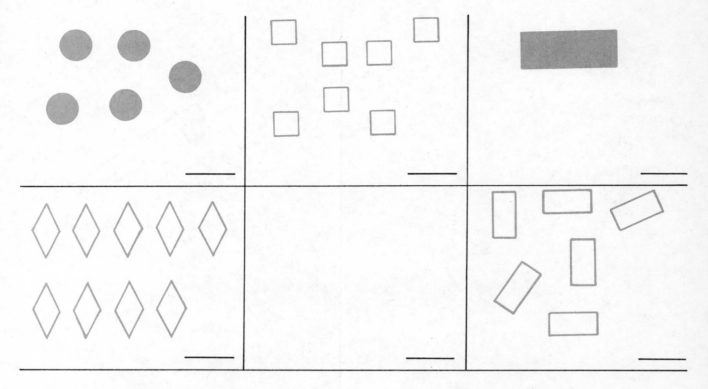

| _____ | _____ | _____ |
| _____ | _____ | _____ |

Read the numeral. Draw that many X's.

7	4	3
10	2	8

Perfect score: 12   My score: _____

Lesson 1   Sums Through 3

Add.

$1 + 1 = \underline{2}$

$\begin{array}{r} 1 \\ +1 \\ \hline 2 \end{array}$

$2 + 1 = \underline{}$

$\begin{array}{r} 2 \\ +1 \\ \hline \end{array}$

$1 + 2 = \underline{}$

$\begin{array}{r} 1 \\ +2 \\ \hline \end{array}$

$2 + 0 = \underline{}$

$\begin{array}{r} 2 \\ +0 \\ \hline \end{array}$

$0 + 2 = \underline{}$

$\begin{array}{r} 0 \\ +2 \\ \hline \end{array}$

$3 + 0 = \underline{}$

$\begin{array}{r} 3 \\ +0 \\ \hline \end{array}$

$0 + 3 = \underline{}$

$\begin{array}{r} 0 \\ +3 \\ \hline \end{array}$

$0 + 0 = \underline{}$

$\begin{array}{r} 0 \\ +0 \\ \hline \end{array}$

$1 + 0 = \underline{}$

$\begin{array}{r} 1 \\ +0 \\ \hline \end{array}$

$0 + 1 = \underline{}$

$\begin{array}{r} 0 \\ +1 \\ \hline \end{array}$

Perfect score: 20   My score: _____

Lesson 2   Sums of 4 and 5

NAME _____

Add.

$\begin{array}{r} 4 \\ +1 \\ \hline 5 \end{array}$

4 + 1 = **5**

$\begin{array}{r} 2 \\ +3 \\ \hline \end{array}$

2 + 3 = _____

$\begin{array}{r} 1 \\ +4 \\ \hline \end{array}$

1 + 4 = _____

$\begin{array}{r} 3 \\ +2 \\ \hline \end{array}$

3 + 2 = _____

$\begin{array}{r} 2 \\ +2 \\ \hline \end{array}$

2 + 2 = _____

$\begin{array}{r} 4 \\ +0 \\ \hline \end{array}$

4 + 0 = _____

$\begin{array}{r} 0 \\ +4 \\ \hline \end{array}$

0 + 4 = _____

$\begin{array}{r} 0 \\ +5 \\ \hline \end{array}$

0 + 5 = _____

$\begin{array}{r} 1 \\ +3 \\ \hline \end{array}$

1 + 3 = _____

$\begin{array}{r} 5 \\ +0 \\ \hline \end{array}$

5 + 0 = _____

$\begin{array}{r} 3 \\ +1 \\ \hline \end{array}$

3 + 1 = _____

Perfect score: 22   My score: _____

12

Lesson 5   Number Families

Add or subtract.

2	1	3	3
+1	+2	−2	−1
3	3	1	

1	3	4	4
+3	+1	−1	−3

2	3	5	5
+3	+2	−2	−3

4	1	5	5
+1	+4	−4	−1

1	2
+1	−1

2	4
+2	−2

2	0	2	2
+0	+2	−2	−0

5	0	5	5
+0	+5	−5	−0

Perfect score: 28   My score: _____

15

Lesson 6   Penny and Nickel

1 penny   5 pennies   1 nickel
1¢   5¢   5¢

Tell how much money.

 5 ¢    _____ ¢

 _____ ¢    _____ ¢

 _____ ¢   _____ ¢

 _____ ¢    _____ ¢

Perfect score: 8   My score: _____

Lesson 7   Problem Solving

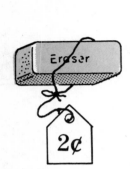 2¢    4¢   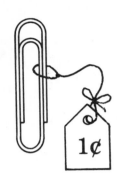 1¢    3¢

Add or subtract.

I buy 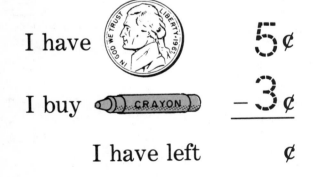	1 ¢	I buy	¢
I buy	+3 ¢	I buy	+ ¢
I spent	4 ¢	I spent	¢

I buy	¢	I buy	¢
I buy	+ ¢	I buy	+ ¢
I spent	¢	I spent	¢

I have	5 ¢	I have	¢
I buy	−3 ¢	I buy	− ¢
I have left	¢	I have left	¢

Perfect score: 6   My score: _____

Chapter 2 Checkup

Add.

3 +1	1 +1	0 +0	2 +1	5 +0	1 +0
0 +3	2 +2	1 +2	0 +1	1 +4	3 +2
1 +3	4 +0	0 +5	2 +0	4 +1	2 +3

Subtract.

2 −1	4 −1	5 −0	3 −2	5 −4	4 −4
4 −0	5 −1	0 −0	4 −2	3 −0	5 −2
2 −0	4 −3	5 −3	3 −1	3 −3	1 −1

Perfect score: 36   My score: _____

Lesson 1   Sums of 6

Add.

$$\begin{array}{r} 1 \\ +5 \\ \hline 6 \end{array}$$

1 + 5 = _6___

$$\begin{array}{r} 2 \\ +4 \\ \hline \end{array}$$

2 + 4 = _____

$$\begin{array}{r} 5 \\ +1 \\ \hline \end{array}$$

5 + 1 = _____

$$\begin{array}{r} 4 \\ +2 \\ \hline \end{array}$$

4 + 2 = _____

$$\begin{array}{r} 6 \\ +0 \\ \hline \end{array}$$

6 + 0 = _____

$$\begin{array}{r} 0 \\ +6 \\ \hline \end{array}$$

0 + 6 = _____

$$\begin{array}{r} 3 \\ +3 \\ \hline \end{array}$$

3 + 3 = _____

$$\begin{array}{r} 2 \\ +4 \\ \hline \end{array}$$
$$\begin{array}{r} 1 \\ +3 \\ \hline \end{array}$$
$$\begin{array}{r} 5 \\ +1 \\ \hline \end{array}$$
$$\begin{array}{r} 3 \\ +3 \\ \hline \end{array}$$
$$\begin{array}{r} 2 \\ +2 \\ \hline \end{array}$$
$$\begin{array}{r} 3 \\ +2 \\ \hline \end{array}$$

Perfect score: 20   My score: _____

Lesson 2 Subtracting from 6

Subtract.

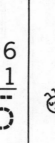

$$\begin{array}{r} 6 \\ -1 \\ \hline 5 \end{array}$$

$6 - 1 = \underline{}$

$$\begin{array}{r} 6 \\ -5 \\ \hline \end{array}$$

$6 - 5 = \underline{}$

$$\begin{array}{r} 6 \\ -4 \\ \hline \end{array}$$

$6 - 4 = \underline{}$

$$\begin{array}{r} 6 \\ -2 \\ \hline \end{array}$$

$6 - 2 = \underline{}$

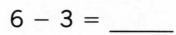

$$\begin{array}{r} 6 \\ -3 \\ \hline \end{array}$$

$6 - 3 = \underline{}$

$$\begin{array}{r} 6 \\ -0 \\ \hline \end{array}$$

$6 - 0 = \underline{}$

$$\begin{array}{r} 6 \\ -3 \\ \hline \end{array} \qquad \begin{array}{r} 6 \\ -6 \\ \hline \end{array} \qquad \begin{array}{r} 6 \\ -1 \\ \hline \end{array} \qquad \begin{array}{r} 6 \\ -4 \\ \hline \end{array} \qquad \begin{array}{r} 6 \\ -2 \\ \hline \end{array} \qquad \begin{array}{r} 6 \\ -5 \\ \hline \end{array}$$

Perfect score: 18   My score: _____

Lesson 3 Sums of 7

Add.

$$3 + 4 = \underline{7}$$

$$\begin{array}{r} 3 \\ +4 \\ \hline 7 \end{array}$$

$$\begin{array}{r} 6 \\ +1 \\ \hline \end{array}$$

$$6 + 1 = \underline{}$$

$$4 + 3 = \underline{}$$

$$\begin{array}{r} 4 \\ +3 \\ \hline \end{array}$$

$$\begin{array}{r} 1 \\ +6 \\ \hline \end{array}$$

$$1 + 6 = \underline{}$$

$$7 + 0 = \underline{}$$

$$\begin{array}{r} 7 \\ +0 \\ \hline \end{array}$$

$$\begin{array}{r} 2 \\ +5 \\ \hline \end{array}$$

$$2 + 5 = \underline{}$$

$$0 + 7 = \underline{}$$

$$\begin{array}{r} 0 \\ +7 \\ \hline \end{array}$$

$$\begin{array}{r} 5 \\ +2 \\ \hline \end{array}$$

$$5 + 2 = \underline{}$$

$$\begin{array}{r} 5 \\ +2 \\ \hline \end{array} \qquad \begin{array}{r} 3 \\ +3 \\ \hline \end{array} \qquad \begin{array}{r} 4 \\ +3 \\ \hline \end{array} \qquad \begin{array}{r} 1 \\ +6 \\ \hline \end{array} \qquad \begin{array}{r} 3 \\ +4 \\ \hline \end{array} \qquad \begin{array}{r} 6 \\ +0 \\ \hline \end{array}$$

Perfect score: 22   My score: _____

Lesson 4 Subtracting from 7

Subtract.

$$7 - 6 = \underline{}$$

$$\begin{array}{r} 7 \\ -6 \\ \hline \end{array}$$

$$7 - 1 = \underline{}$$

$$\begin{array}{r} 7 \\ -1 \\ \hline \end{array}$$

$$7 - 3 = \underline{}$$

$$\begin{array}{r} 7 \\ -3 \\ \hline \end{array}$$

$$7 - 4 = \underline{}$$

$$\begin{array}{r} 7 \\ -4 \\ \hline \end{array}$$

$$7 - 7 = \underline{}$$

$$\begin{array}{r} 7 \\ -7 \\ \hline \end{array}$$

$$7 - 0 = \underline{}$$

$$\begin{array}{r} 7 \\ -0 \\ \hline \end{array}$$

$$7 - 2 = \underline{}$$

$$\begin{array}{r} 7 \\ -2 \\ \hline \end{array}$$

$$7 - 5 = \underline{}$$

$$\begin{array}{r} 7 \\ -5 \\ \hline \end{array}$$

Perfect score: 16   My score: _____

Lesson 5 Sums of 8

Add.

5 + 3 = __8__

$$\begin{array}{r} 5 \\ +3 \\ \hline 8 \end{array}$$

$$\begin{array}{r} 7 \\ +1 \\ \hline \end{array}$$

7 + 1 = _____

3 + 5 = _____

$$\begin{array}{r} 3 \\ +5 \\ \hline \end{array}$$

$$\begin{array}{r} 1 \\ +7 \\ \hline \end{array}$$

1 + 7 = _____

2 + 6 = _____

$$\begin{array}{r} 2 \\ +6 \\ \hline \end{array}$$

$$\begin{array}{r} 6 \\ +2 \\ \hline \end{array}$$

6 + 2 = _____

$$\begin{array}{r} 4 \\ +4 \\ \hline \end{array}$$

4 + 4 = _____

$$\begin{array}{r} 3 \\ +3 \\ \hline \end{array}$$
$$\begin{array}{r} 5 \\ +3 \\ \hline \end{array}$$
$$\begin{array}{r} 2 \\ +6 \\ \hline \end{array}$$
$$\begin{array}{r} 8 \\ +0 \\ \hline \end{array}$$
$$\begin{array}{r} 4 \\ +3 \\ \hline \end{array}$$
$$\begin{array}{r} 0 \\ +8 \\ \hline \end{array}$$

Perfect score: 20   My score: _____

Lesson 6　Subtracting from 8

Subtract.

$$\begin{array}{r} 8 \\ -7 \\ \hline \end{array}$$

8 − 7 = _____

$$\begin{array}{r} 8 \\ -1 \\ \hline \end{array}$$

8 − 1 = _____

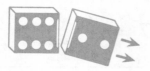

$$\begin{array}{r} 8 \\ -2 \\ \hline \end{array}$$

8 − 2 = _____

$$\begin{array}{r} 8 \\ -6 \\ \hline \end{array}$$

8 − 6 = _____

$$\begin{array}{r} 8 \\ -4 \\ \hline \end{array}$$

8 − 4 = _____

$$\begin{array}{r} 8 \\ -8 \\ \hline \end{array}$$

8 − 8 = _____

$$\begin{array}{r} 8 \\ -3 \\ \hline \end{array}$$

8 − 3 = _____

$$\begin{array}{r} 8 \\ -5 \\ \hline \end{array}$$

8 − 5 = _____

Perfect score: 16　My score: _____

Lesson 7   Addition and Subtraction

Add.

5 +3	1 +6	3 +3	2 +6	1 +7	5 +1
0 +7	4 +2	4 +4	6 +0	3 +4	6 +1
3 +5	8 +0	5 +2	2 +4	6 +2	0 +8

Subtract.

8 −3	6 −5	8 −4	7 −3	6 −2	6 −6
8 −5	7 −0	8 −1	7 −6	8 −6	7 −5
8 −8	6 −3	7 −1	8 −2	6 −1	7 −2

Perfect score: 36   My score: _____

Problem Solving

Solve each problem.

There are 6 blue .

There are 2 white .

How many in all?

$$\begin{array}{r} 6 \\ +\ 2 \\ \hline 8 \end{array}$$

There are 7 .

4 fly away.

How many are left?

$$\begin{array}{r} 7 \\ -\ 4 \\ \hline \end{array}$$

I saw 2 big  .

I saw 3 little  .

How many in all?

$$\begin{array}{r} 2 \\ +\ 3 \\ \hline \end{array}$$

Bob has 8 .

Ann has 5 .

How many more does Bob have than Ann?

$$\begin{array}{r} 8 \\ -\ 5 \\ \hline \end{array}$$

There is 1 .

Then 5 more come.

Now how many in all?

$$\begin{array}{r} 1 \\ +\ 5 \\ \hline \end{array}$$

Perfect score: 5   My score: _____

Lesson 8   Addition and Subtraction

Add or subtract.   STOP!   Watch the + and −.

2 +5	8 −3	7 +0	8 −4	6 +1	7 −2
7 −5	3 +3	4 +2	0 +6	8 −0	8 −6
8 −1	7 −1	1 +6	6 −5	3 +4	5 +1
6 −6	2 +4	5 +2	6 −0	1 +7	7 −3
1 +5	6 −3	7 −4	4 +3	8 −2	4 +4
7 −6	5 +3	6 −2	0 +8	2 +6	8 −8

Perfect score: 36   My score: _____

Problem Solving

Solve each problem.

There are 8 🐰 .

Then 7 ran away.

How many are left?

$$\begin{array}{r} 8 \\ -\ 7 \\ \hline \end{array}$$

There are 4 white ☂ .

There are 3 blue ☂ .

How many in all?

$$\begin{array}{r} 4 \\ +\ 3 \\ \hline \end{array}$$

Rob saw 7 🐦 flying.

He saw 1 🐦 sitting.

How many did he see in all?

Cal has 6 🤖 .

He gave Ann 4 🤖 .

How many does he have left?

There are 7 🎈 .

7 of the 🎈 broke.

How many are left?

Lesson 9   Addition and Subtraction

NAME _____

Add or subtract.
If you get 6, color that part orange.

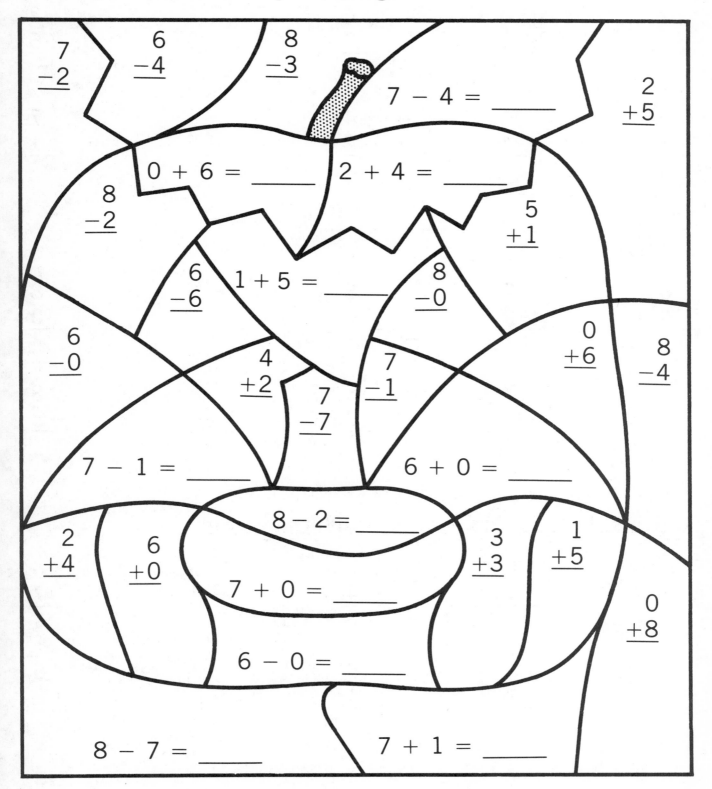

$$7 - 4 = \underline{\hspace{1.5cm}}$$

$$0 + 6 = \underline{\hspace{1.5cm}}$$

$$2 + 4 = \underline{\hspace{1.5cm}}$$

$$1 + 5 = \underline{\hspace{1.5cm}}$$

$$7 - 1 = \underline{\hspace{1.5cm}}$$

$$6 + 0 = \underline{\hspace{1.5cm}}$$

$$8 - 2 = \underline{\hspace{1.5cm}}$$

$$7 + 0 = \underline{\hspace{1.5cm}}$$

$$6 - 0 = \underline{\hspace{1.5cm}}$$

$$8 - 7 = \underline{\hspace{1.5cm}}$$

$$7 + 1 = \underline{\hspace{1.5cm}}$$

$$\begin{array}{r} 7 \\ -2 \\ \hline \end{array}$$

$$\begin{array}{r} 6 \\ -4 \\ \hline \end{array}$$

$$\begin{array}{r} 8 \\ -3 \\ \hline \end{array}$$

$$\begin{array}{r} 2 \\ +5 \\ \hline \end{array}$$

$$\begin{array}{r} 8 \\ -2 \\ \hline \end{array}$$

$$\begin{array}{r} 5 \\ +1 \\ \hline \end{array}$$

$$\begin{array}{r} 6 \\ -6 \\ \hline \end{array}$$

$$\begin{array}{r} 8 \\ -0 \\ \hline \end{array}$$

$$\begin{array}{r} 6 \\ -0 \\ \hline \end{array}$$

$$\begin{array}{r} 4 \\ +2 \\ \hline \end{array}$$

$$\begin{array}{r} 7 \\ -1 \\ \hline \end{array}$$

$$\begin{array}{r} 0 \\ +6 \\ \hline \end{array}$$

$$\begin{array}{r} 8 \\ -4 \\ \hline \end{array}$$

$$\begin{array}{r} 7 \\ -7 \\ \hline \end{array}$$

$$\begin{array}{r} 2 \\ +4 \\ \hline \end{array}$$

$$\begin{array}{r} 6 \\ +0 \\ \hline \end{array}$$

$$\begin{array}{r} 3 \\ +3 \\ \hline \end{array}$$

$$\begin{array}{r} 1 \\ +5 \\ \hline \end{array}$$

$$\begin{array}{r} 0 \\ +8 \\ \hline \end{array}$$

Perfect score: 30   My score: _____

29

Add.

3	0	4	2	2
+5	+6	+3	+5	+6

5	4	4	1	7
+1	+4	+2	+6	+1

Subtract.

6	7	8	6	8
−4	−2	−6	−3	−0

8	7	6	6	8
−1	−5	−2	−0	−3

Add or subtract.   Watch the + and −.

3	6	7	3	8
+3	−1	−4	+4	−7

7	5	8	7	6
−7	+2	−4	+0	+2

Perfect score: 30   My score: _____

Lesson 1   Sums of 9

Add.

$$\begin{array}{r} 2 \\ +7 \\ \hline 9 \end{array}$$

2 + 7 = __9__

$$\begin{array}{r} 7 \\ +2 \\ \hline \end{array}$$

7 + 2 = ____

$$\begin{array}{r} 5 \\ +4 \\ \hline \end{array}$$

5 + 4 = ____

$$\begin{array}{r} 4 \\ +5 \\ \hline \end{array}$$

4 + 5 = ____

$$\begin{array}{r} 1 \\ +8 \\ \hline \end{array}$$

1 + 8 = ____

$$\begin{array}{r} 8 \\ +1 \\ \hline \end{array}$$

8 + 1 = ____

$$\begin{array}{r} 3 \\ +6 \\ \hline \end{array}$$

3 + 6 = ____

$$\begin{array}{r} 6 \\ +3 \\ \hline \end{array}$$

6 + 3 = ____

$$\begin{array}{r} 0 \\ +9 \\ \hline \end{array}$$

0 + 9 = ____

$$\begin{array}{r} 9 \\ +0 \\ \hline \end{array}$$

9 + 0 = ____

$$\begin{array}{r} 5 \\ +4 \\ \hline \end{array} \qquad \begin{array}{r} 3 \\ +6 \\ \hline \end{array} \qquad \begin{array}{r} 8 \\ +1 \\ \hline \end{array} \qquad \begin{array}{r} 4 \\ +5 \\ \hline \end{array} \qquad \begin{array}{r} 7 \\ +2 \\ \hline \end{array} \qquad \begin{array}{r} 0 \\ +8 \\ \hline \end{array}$$

Perfect score: 26   My score: _____

Lesson 2 Subtracting from 9

Subtract.

9 − 6 = __3__

$$\begin{array}{r} 9 \\ -6 \\ \hline 3 \end{array}$$

9 − 3 = _____

$$\begin{array}{r} 9 \\ -3 \\ \hline \end{array}$$

9 − 0 = _____

$$\begin{array}{r} 9 \\ -0 \\ \hline \end{array}$$

9 − 9 = _____

$$\begin{array}{r} 9 \\ -9 \\ \hline \end{array}$$

9 − 5 = _____

$$\begin{array}{r} 9 \\ -5 \\ \hline \end{array}$$

9 − 4 = _____

$$\begin{array}{r} 9 \\ -4 \\ \hline \end{array}$$

9 − 8 = _____

$$\begin{array}{r} 9 \\ -8 \\ \hline \end{array}$$

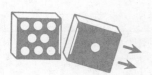

9 − 1 = _____

$$\begin{array}{r} 9 \\ -1 \\ \hline \end{array}$$

9 − 2 = _____

$$\begin{array}{r} 9 \\ -2 \\ \hline \end{array}$$

9 − 7 = _____

$$\begin{array}{r} 9 \\ -7 \\ \hline \end{array}$$

Perfect score: 20   My score: _____

Lesson 3   Sums of 10

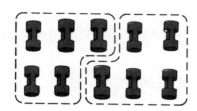

$$5 + 5 = \underline{10}$$

$$\begin{array}{r} 5 \\ +5 \\ \hline 10 \end{array}$$

Add.

$$7 + 3 = \underline{10}$$

$$\begin{array}{r} 7 \\ +3 \\ \hline 10 \end{array}$$

$$3 + 7 = \underline{}$$

$$\begin{array}{r} 3 \\ +7 \\ \hline \end{array}$$

$1 + 9 = \underline{}$ $\begin{array}{r} 1 \\ +9 \\ \hline \end{array}$ $\begin{array}{r} 9 \\ +1 \\ \hline \end{array}$

$9 + 1 = \underline{}$

$2 + 8 = \underline{}$ $\begin{array}{r} 2 \\ +8 \\ \hline \end{array}$ $\begin{array}{r} 8 \\ +2 \\ \hline \end{array}$

$8 + 2 = \underline{}$

$6 + 4 = \underline{}$ $\begin{array}{r} 6 \\ +4 \\ \hline \end{array}$ $\begin{array}{r} 4 \\ +6 \\ \hline \end{array}$

$4 + 6 = \underline{}$

$10 + 0 = \underline{}$ $\begin{array}{r} 10 \\ + \, 0 \\ \hline \end{array}$ $\begin{array}{r} 0 \\ +10 \\ \hline \end{array}$

$0 + 10 = \underline{}$

$\begin{array}{r} 3 \\ +7 \\ \hline \end{array}$ $\begin{array}{r} 6 \\ +2 \\ \hline \end{array}$ $\begin{array}{r} 5 \\ +5 \\ \hline \end{array}$ $\begin{array}{r} 1 \\ +9 \\ \hline \end{array}$ $\begin{array}{r} 2 \\ +8 \\ \hline \end{array}$ $\begin{array}{r} 7 \\ +2 \\ \hline \end{array}$

Perfect score: 26   My score: _____

Lesson 4 Subtracting from 10

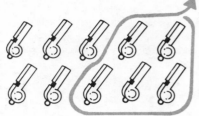

$$\begin{array}{r} 1\,0 \\ -\ 5 \\ \hline 5 \end{array}$$

10 − 5 = __5__

$$\begin{array}{r} 1\,0 \\ -1\,0 \\ \hline 0 \end{array}$$

10 − 10 = __0__

Subtract.

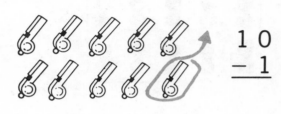

$$\begin{array}{r} 1\,0 \\ -\ 1 \end{array}$$

10 − 1 = _____

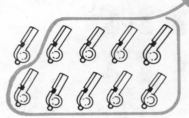

$$\begin{array}{r} 1\,0 \\ -\ 9 \end{array}$$

10 − 9 = _____

10 − 7 = _____ $\begin{array}{r} 1\,0 \\ -\ 7 \\ \hline \end{array}$ $\begin{array}{r} 1\,0 \\ -\ 3 \\ \hline \end{array}$

10 − 4 = _____ $\begin{array}{r} 1\,0 \\ -\ 4 \\ \hline \end{array}$ $\begin{array}{r} 1\,0 \\ -\ 6 \\ \hline \end{array}$

10 − 3 = _____

10 − 6 = _____

10 − 8 = _____ $\begin{array}{r} 1\,0 \\ -\ 8 \\ \hline \end{array}$ $\begin{array}{r} 1\,0 \\ -\ 2 \\ \hline \end{array}$

10 − 0 = _____ $\begin{array}{r} 1\,0 \\ -\ 0 \\ \hline \end{array}$

10 − 2 = _____

$$\begin{array}{r} 1\,0 \\ -\ 7 \\ \hline \end{array}$$
$$\begin{array}{r} 1\,0 \\ -\ 1 \\ \hline \end{array}$$
$$\begin{array}{r} 1\,0 \\ -\ 5 \\ \hline \end{array}$$
$$\begin{array}{r} 1\,0 \\ -1\,0 \\ \hline \end{array}$$
$$\begin{array}{r} 1\,0 \\ -\ 2 \\ \hline \end{array}$$
$$\begin{array}{r} 1\,0 \\ -\ 6 \\ \hline \end{array}$$

Perfect score: 24   My score: _____

Lesson 5   Practicing Addition

Add.

6 +4	7 +2	4 +4	4 +5	9 +1	3 +2
2 +7	6 +2	9 +0	2 +5	1 +4	4 +6
8 +1	2 +2	3 +6	1 +7	7 +3	1 +8
2 +3	2 +8	3 +5	8 +2	6 +1	0 +9
1 +9	6 +3	3 +4	5 +2	5 +4	4 +3
5 +3	8 +0	5 +5	3 +7	2 +6	3 +3

Perfect score: 36   My score: _____

Problem Solving

Solve each problem.

There are 5 white .

There are 4 blue .

How many in all?

There are 3 .

7 more come.

How many are there now?

Beth has 9 .

She buys 1 more.

Now how many does she have?

There are 6 ☐ .

There are 3 ☐ .

How many in all?

There were 8 🐕 .

2 more came.

Then how many were there?

Lesson 6   Practicing Subtraction

Subtract.

9 −4	7 −6	1 0 − 5	9 −7	8 −5	1 0 −9
1 0 −4	6 −3	9 −6	1 0 − 3	9 −0	5 −1
3 −1	9 −1	1 0 − 8	7 −2	9 −5	2 −2
1 0 − 1	7 −0	5 −3	8 −7	1 0 − 2	6 −4
9 −8	7 −4	1 0 − 0	4 −2	8 −4	9 −3
1 0 − 6	8 −6	9 −2	8 −1	9 −9	1 0 − 7

Perfect score: 36   My score: _____

Problem Solving

Solve each problem.

There are 10 white 🌼.

There are 4 blue 🌸.

How many more white 🌼 than blue 🌸 are there?

$$\begin{array}{r} 10 \\ -4 \\ \hline \end{array}$$

---

10 BLUE are on the table.

2 are broken.

How many are not broken?

There are 9 🐟.

6 swim away.

How many 🐟 are left?

Joni wants 9 🪙.

She has 5 🪙.

How many more does she need?

There were 10 ☃.

5 ☃ melted.

How many did not melt?

Perfect score: 5   My score: _____

38

Lesson 7   Addition and Subtraction

Add or subtract. Watch the + and −.

5 +2	1 0 − 6	7 +1	9 −4	1 +9	9 −8
9 +0	8 −0	1 0 − 9	1 +8	2 +7	9 −1
1 0 − 1	2 +8	1 +6	8 −3	6 +3	1 0 − 3
9 −9	4 +5	8 +1	1 0 − 8	9 −0	5 +5
4 +4	9 −3	7 +3	9 −7	3 +6	1 0 − 7
7 +2	8 −7	0 +8	9 −2	1 0 − 5	4 +6

Perfect score: 36   My score: _____

Problem Solving

Solve each problem.

There are 9 white ⚪ .

There are 4 blue 🔵 .

How many more white ⚪ than blue 🔵 ?

$$\begin{array}{r} 9 \\ -\ 4 \\ \hline \end{array}$$

Ben has 7 🍁 .

He finds 2 more.

Now how many does he have?

$$\begin{array}{r} 7 \\ +\ 2 \\ \hline \end{array}$$

There are 5 ⬜ .

There are 5 ⬛ .

How many in all?

There were 10 🐈 .

6 ran away.

Then how many were there?

There were 9 🍞 .

8 were eaten.

How many were not eaten?

Perfect score: 5   My score: _____

40

Lesson 8   Money

1 penny
1¢

1 nickel
5¢

1 dime
10¢

Tell how much money.

_____ ¢

_____ ¢

_____ ¢

_____ ¢

_____ ¢

_____ ¢

_____ ¢

_____ ¢

Perfect score: 8   My score: _____

41

Problem Solving

10 pennies   10¢

1 dime
10¢

I have	I buy	I have left
	5¢	9 ¢ − 5 ¢ ¢
	6¢	¢ − ¢ ¢
	8¢	¢ − ¢ ¢
	5¢	¢ − ¢ ¢

Perfect score: 4   My score: _____

42

Lesson 9   Problem Solving

3¢   4¢   5¢   6¢

Add or subtract.

I buy   3¢

I buy   + 4¢

 I spent   ¢

I buy   ¢

I buy   +   ¢

 I spent   ¢

 I have   1 0¢

I buy   − 6¢

 I have left   ¢

 I have   9¢

I buy   −   ¢

 I have left   ¢

 I have   8¢

I buy   −   ¢

 I have left   ¢

 I have   1 0¢

I buy   −   ¢

 I have left   ¢

Perfect score: 6   My score: _____

43

Chapter 4   Checkup

Add.

6 +2	8 +1	4 +6	7 +3	2 +8

5 +4	6 +3	1 +9	3 +6	9 +0

Subtract.

1 0 − 4	9 −2	9 −6	1 0 − 3	1 0 − 1

9 −1	9 −5	1 0 − 9	9 −7	1 0 − 5

Add or subtract.   Watch the + and −.

0 +8	1 0 − 8	9 −0	2 +7	9 −9

1 0 − 2	8 +2	1 0 − 6	3 +7	5 +5

Perfect score: 30   My score: _____

$\underline{\quad 1 \quad}$ ten $\underline{\quad 0 \quad}$ ones $= \underline{\quad 10 \quad}$

$\underline{\quad 1 \quad}$ ten $\underline{\quad 1 \quad}$ one $= \underline{\quad 11 \quad}$

Complete.

_____ ten _____ ones = _____

_____ ten _____ ones = _____

_____ ten _____ ones = _____

_____ ten _____ ones = _____

_____ ten _____ ones = _____

_____ ten _____ ones = _____

_____ ten _____ ones = _____

_____ ten _____ ones = _____

_____ ten _____ ones = _____

Perfect score: 24   My score: _____

Lesson 2 Numbers 20 Through 29

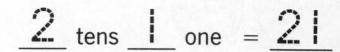
__2__ tens __0__ ones = __20__

__2__ tens __1__ one = __21__

Complete.

  ___ tens ___ ones = ____

  ___ tens ___ ones = ____

  ___ tens ___ ones = ____

  ___ tens ___ ones = ____

  ___ tens ___ ones = ____

  ___ tens ___ ones = ____

  ___ tens ___ ones = ____

  ___ tens ___ ones = ____

Perfect score: 24   My score: _____

Lesson 3 Numbers 10 Through 29

Complete.

2 tens **3** ones = **23**   ____ tens ____ ones = _____

____ ten ____ ones = _____   ____ tens ____ ones = _____

____ tens ____ ones = _____   ____ ten ____ ones = _____

____ ten ____ ones = _____   ____ tens ____ ones = _____

Perfect score: 24   My score: _____

47

Lesson 4 Tens

$\underline{\text{1}}$ ten = $\underline{\text{10}}$

$\underline{\text{2}}$ tens = **20**

Complete.

_____ tens = _____

_____ tens = _____

_____ tens = _____

_____ tens = _____

_____ tens = _____

_____ tens = _____

_____ tens = _____

Perfect score: 14   My score: _____

Lesson 5   Numbers 30 Through 49
Complete.

____3____ tens ____2____ ones = ____32____

____ tens ____ ones = ____

____ tens ____ ones = ____

____ tens ____ ones = ____

3 tens 7 ones = _37_

4 tens 1 one = _____

4 tens 9 ones = _____

3 tens 5 ones = _____

4 tens 3 ones = _____

4 tens 2 ones = _____

3 tens 3 ones = _____

4 tens 4 ones = _____

4 tens 6 ones = _____

3 tens 8 ones = _____

Perfect score: 22   My score: _____

Numbers 0 Through 49

Complete the table.

0	1	2							9
10					15				
		22					27		
			33						
				44					49

Connect the dots in order.

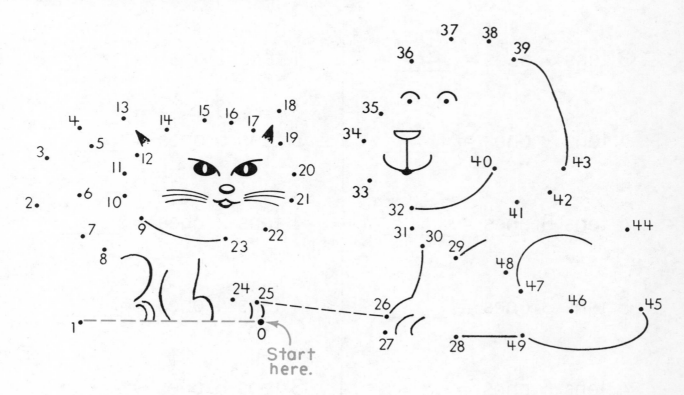

Start here.

Perfect score: 51   My score: _____

50

Lesson 6   Numbers 50 Through 69

6 tens 4 ones = ___64___

Complete.

5 tens 0 ones = __50__

5 tens 1 one = _____

5 tens 2 ones = _____

5 tens 3 ones = _____

5 tens 4 ones = _____

5 tens 5 ones = _____

5 tens 6 ones = _____

5 tens 7 ones = _____

5 tens 8 ones = _____

5 tens 9 ones = _____

6 tens 0 ones = _____

6 tens 1 one = _____

6 tens 2 ones = _____

6 tens 3 ones = _____

6 tens 4 ones = _____

6 tens 5 ones = _____

6 tens 6 ones = _____

6 tens 7 ones = _____

6 tens 8 ones = _____

6 tens 9 ones = _____

Perfect score: 20   My score: _____

Lesson 7   Numbers 70 Through 99

8 tens 6 ones = ___86___   9 tens 4 ones = ___94___

Complete.

7 tens 4 ones = _____   8 tens 8 ones = _____

9 tens 1 one = _____   7 tens 9 ones = _____

7 tens 8 ones = _____   8 tens 7 ones = _____

9 tens 8 ones = _____   8 tens 9 ones = _____

8 tens 5 ones = _____   9 tens 2 ones = _____

9 tens 9 ones = _____   7 tens 3 ones = _____

7 tens 0 ones = _____   9 tens 6 ones = _____

Perfect score: 14   My score: _____

Lesson 8   Numbers 50 Through 99

Tell how many cents.

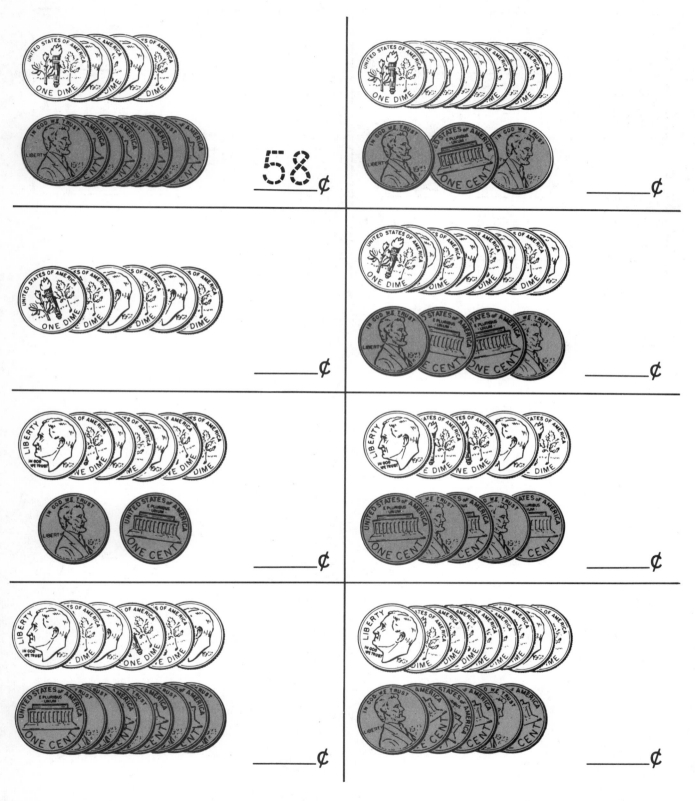

58 ¢

_____ ¢

_____ ¢

_____ ¢

_____ ¢

_____ ¢

_____ ¢

_____ ¢

Perfect score: 8   My score: _____

Numbers 50 Through 99

Complete the table.

50		52						58	
60						66			69
							77		
80			84						
		93							99

Connect the dots in order.

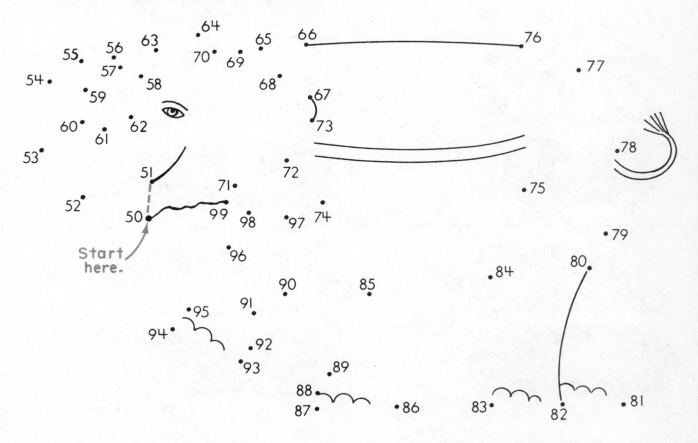

Start here.

Perfect score: 51   My score: _____

54

Lesson 9   Numeration

Ring the largest.
X the smallest.

26 X̶1̶5̶ (31)	53 71 68	40 70 90
32 23 30	85 65 95	64 46 42
84 89 87	91 57 19	78 94 29

Complete.

Before	*Between*	*After*
__18__, 19, 20	36, __37__, 38	91, 92, _____
_____, 64, 65	29, _____, 31	87, 88, _____
_____, 70, 71	53, _____, 55	48, 49, _____
_____, 34, 35	20, _____, 22	66, 67, _____

Perfect score: 30   My score: _____

55

Chapter 5   Checkup

Complete.

1 ten 4 ones = _____   6 tens 0 ones = _____

3 tens 7 ones = _____   9 tens 9 ones = _____

2 tens 8 ones = _____   4 tens 5 ones = _____

8 tens 3 ones = _____   5 tens 4 ones = _____

7 tens 0 ones = _____   3 tens 1 one = _____

9 tens 2 ones = _____   6 tens 6 ones = _____

Name the numbers in order for each row.

16	17							24
42								50
79								87

Perfect score: 36   My score: _____

56

4:00

4 o'clock
4:00

Both clocks show the same time.

Write the time for each clock.

_|_ o'clock

_|_:00

_____ o'clock

_____:00

_____ o'clock

_____:00

4:00

_____ o'clock

_____:_____

5:00

_____ o'clock

_____:_____

6:00

_____ o'clock

_____:_____

_____ o'clock

_____:_____

_____ o'clock

_____:_____

_____ o'clock

_____:_____

Perfect score: 18   My score: _____

Time

Show this time on this clock. Show this time on this clock.

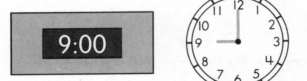

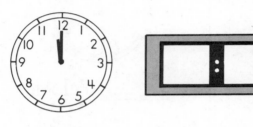

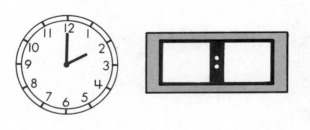

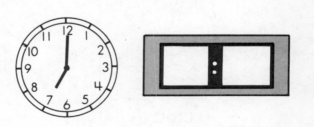

Perfect score: 6   My score: _____

Lesson 2   Time—Half Hour

1 o'clock
1:00

one thirty
1:30

2 o'clock
2:00

Write the time for each clock.

two thirty
2 :30

_____ thirty
___:30

_____ thirty
___:30

| 11:30 | 12:30 | 5:30 |

_____ thirty

___:___

_____ thirty

___:___

_____ thirty

___:___

_____ thirty

___:___

_____ thirty

___:___

_____ thirty

___:___

_____ thirty

___:___

Perfect score: 18   My score: _____

59

Time

Show this time on this clock.

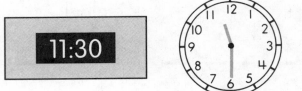
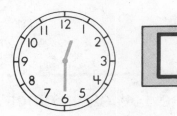

Show this time on this clock.

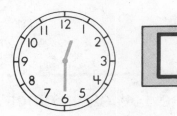

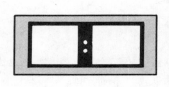

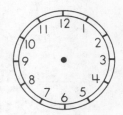

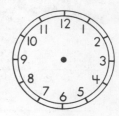

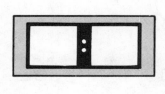

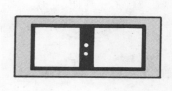

Perfect score: 6   My score: _____

Lesson 3   Calendar

September						
S	M	T	W	Th	F	S
	1	2	3	4	5	6
7	8	9	10	11	12	13
14	15	16	17	18	19	20
21	22	23	24	25	26	27
28	29	30				

There are 12 months in a year.
September has exactly 30 days.
September 1 is on Monday.
There are 5 Mondays in September.
There are 4 Saturdays in September.

September 19 is on _____.

Complete.

How many days are in a week? _____

What day comes after Thursday? _____

September 30 is on _____.

There are _____ Tuesdays in September.

Days of the Week
Sunday
Monday
Tuesday
Wednesday
Thursday
Friday
Saturday

October						
S	M	T	W	Th	F	S
			1	2	3	4
5	6	7	8	9	10	11
12	13	14	15	16	17	18
19	20	21	22	23	24	25
26	27	28	29	30	31	

October has exactly _____ days.

October 1 is on _____.

There are _____ Wednesdays in October.

October 31 is on _____.

There are _____ Sundays in October.

Perfect score: 9   My score: _____

61

Calendar

January						
Sun.	Mon.	Tues.	Wed.	Thurs.	Fri.	Sat.
				1	2	3
4	5	6	7	8	9	10
11	12	13	14	15	16	17
18	19	20	21	22	23	24
25	26	27	28	29	30	31

Months of the Year	Number of Days
January	31
February	28
March	31
April	30
May	31
June	30
July	31
August	31
September	30
October	31
November	30
December	31

Complete.

Thirty days has September,

April, June, and _____.

All the rest have thirty one,

Except _____, which has only 28.

The first month of the year is _____.

The last month of the year is _____.

January has _____ days.

January 3 is on _____.

In what month is your birthday? _____

What month is it today? _____

What month is Valentine's Day in? _____

Perfect score: 9   My score: _____

62

Lesson 4   Problem Solving

March		Our Weather Calendar				
Sun.	Mon.	Tues.	Wed.	Thurs.	Fri.	Sat.
				snowy 1	sunny 2	snowy 3
snowy 4	sunny 5	cloudy 6	sunny 7	sunny 8	cloudy 9	sunny 10
sunny 11	sunny 12	sunny 13	cloudy 14	rainy 15	sunny 16	sunny 17
sunny 18	cloudy 19	cloudy 20	stormy 21	sunny 22	cloudy 23	sunny 24
cloudy 25	rainy 26	sunny 27	stormy 28	rainy 29	cloudy 30	rainy 31

sunny

rainy

cloudy

snowy

stormy

Complete.

What was the weather on

March 4? _____   March 10? _____

March 15? _____   March 21? _____

March 30? _____   March 31? _____

How many days did it rain   ?   _____

How many days did it storm   ?   _____

How many days did it snow   ?   _____

How many days was it cloudy   ?   _____

How many days was it sunny   ?   _____

Perfect score: 11   My score: _____

63

Problem Solving

Make a weather calendar for one week.

Write the numbers to show the dates.

Draw to show the weather.

 sunny

 cloudy

 rainy

 snowy

 stormy

Sunday	Monday	Tuesday	Wednesday	Thursday	Friday	Saturday

Use your weather calendar.

How many days was it

cloudy ? _____   sunny ? _____

snowy ? _____   stormy ? _____

rainy ? _____

Complete.

Write today's date. _____ _____, _____
                        Month   Date   Year

What day of the week is it today? _____

Write your birthdate. _____ _____, _____
                          Month   Date   Year

Perfect score: 19   My score: _____

64

Lesson 5   Centimeter

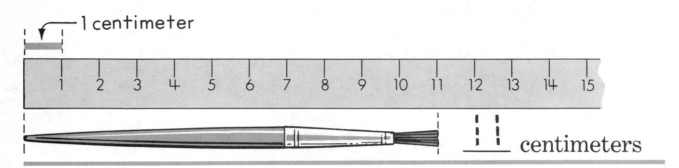

1 centimeter

| | centimeters

How long is each object?

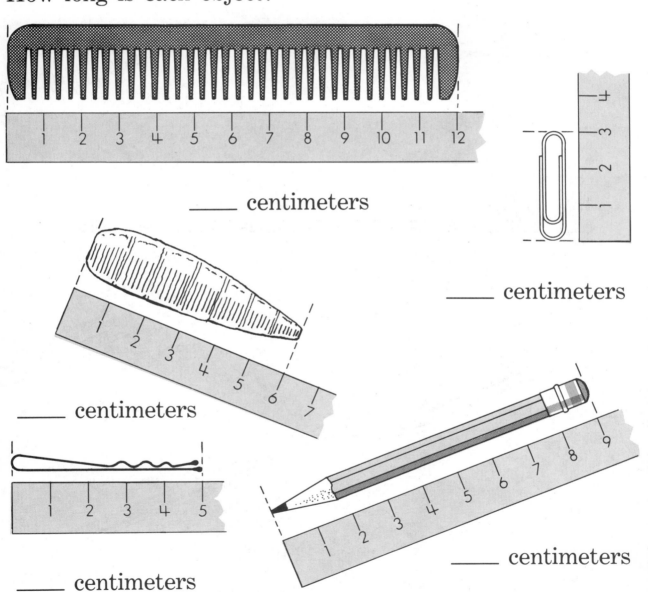

_____ centimeters

_____ centimeters

_____ centimeters

_____ centimeters

_____ centimeters

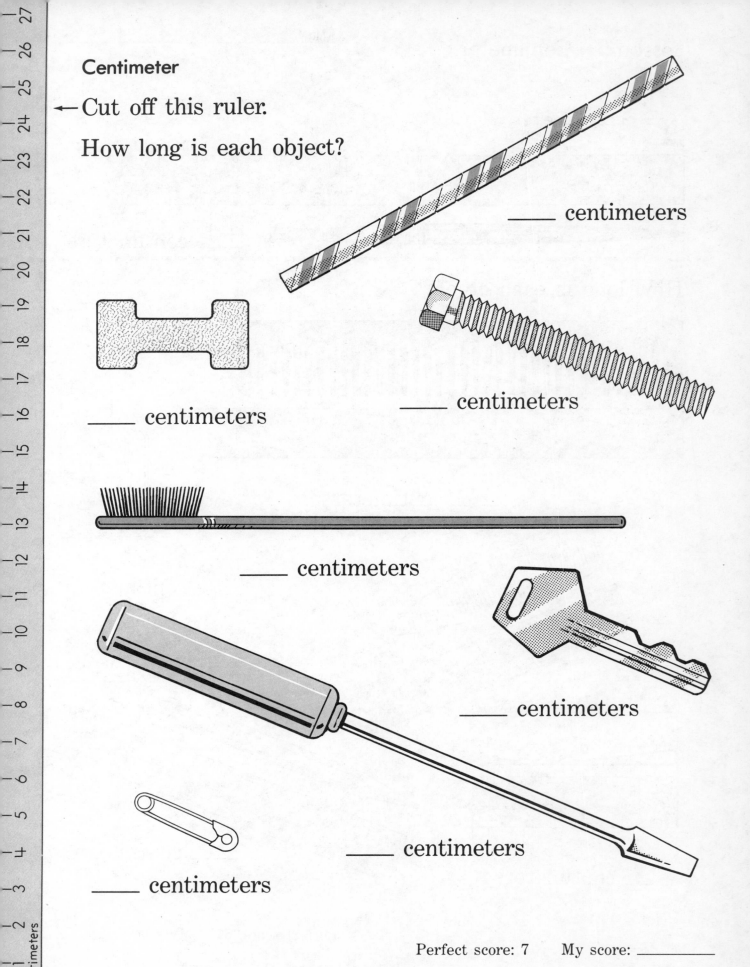

Centimeter

←Cut off this ruler.

How long is each object?

_____ centimeters

_____ centimeters

_____ centimeters

_____ centimeters

_____ centimeters

_____ centimeters

_____ centimeters

Perfect score: 7   My score: _____

66

Lesson 6 Inch

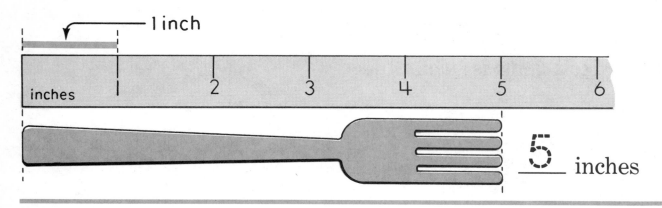

1 inch

_____ 5 inches

How long is each object?

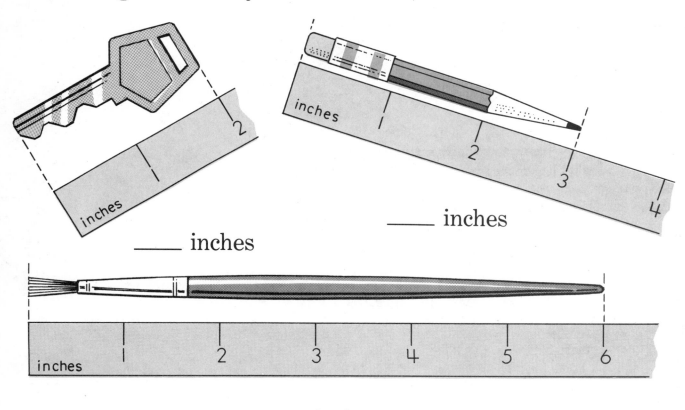

_____ inches

_____ inches

_____ inches

_____ inch

_____ inches

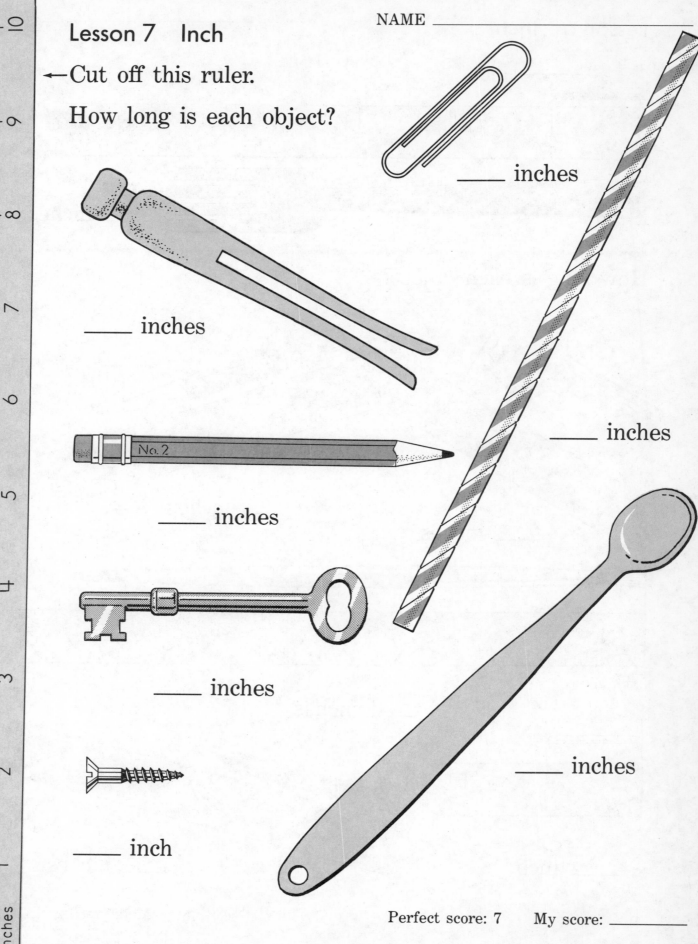

Lesson 7 Inch

←Cut off this ruler.

How long is each object?

_____ inches

_____ inches

_____ inches

_____ inches

_____ inches

_____ inches

_____ inch

inches

Perfect score: 7   My score: _____

Lesson 7   Measuring

Work with a friend.

Use a centimeter ruler.

Measure each other.

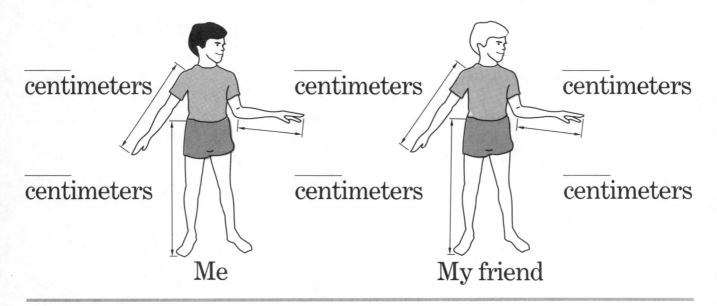

_____ centimeters   _____ centimeters   _____ centimeters

_____ centimeters   _____ centimeters   _____ centimeters

Me   My friend

Use an inch ruler.

Measure each other.

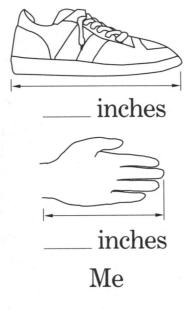

_____ inches

_____ inches

Me

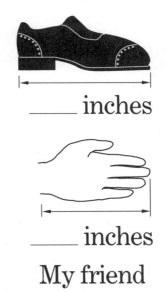

_____ inches

_____ inches

My friend

Perfect score: 10   My score: _____

69

NAME _____

Write the time for each clock.

7:30

_____ thirty

_____ : _____

_____ : _____

How long is each object?

_____ centimeters

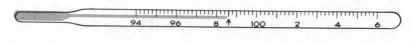

_____ centimeters

Use an inch ruler.
How long is each object?

_____ inches

_____ inch

_____ inches

Perfect score: 8   My score: _____

Lesson 1   Addition and Subtraction

Add.

5 +2	7 +1	3 +7	2 +2	6 +3	3 +2
1 +8	3 +1	1 +1	2 +8	3 +4	5 +4
2 +1	5 +5	9 +1	2 +6	4 +4	1 0 + 0

Subtract.

8 −1	9 −9	6 −3	7 −0	4 −2	1 0 − 3
1 0 − 9	9 −6	7 −6	1 0 − 8	5 −4	9 −2
5 −3	8 −5	1 0 − 6	6 −4	9 −8	7 −4

Perfect score: 36   My score: _____

Addition and Subtraction

Add or subtract.
If you get 5, color
that part green.

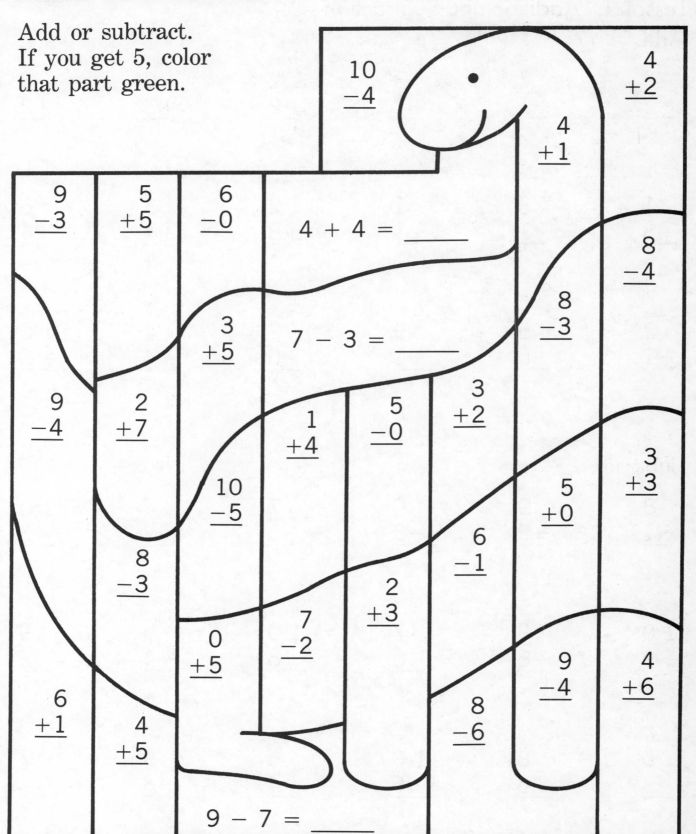

$10 - 4$

$4 + 2$

$4 + 1$

$9 - 3$

$5 + 5$

$6 - 0$

$4 + 4 = \underline{\hspace{1cm}}$

$8 - 4$

$8 - 3$

$3 + 5$

$7 - 3 = \underline{\hspace{1cm}}$

$9 - 4$

$2 + 7$

$1 + 4$

$5 - 0$

$3 + 2$

$10 - 5$

$3 + 3$

$5 + 0$

$6 - 1$

$8 - 3$

$2 + 3$

$0 + 5$

$7 - 2$

$9 - 4$

$4 + 6$

$6 + 1$

$4 + 5$

$8 - 6$

$9 - 7 = \underline{\hspace{1cm}}$

Perfect score: 30   My score: _____

72

Lesson 2 Adding and Subtracting Tens

2 tens	2 0		8 tens	8 0
+6 tens	+6 0		−6 tens	−6 0
8 tens	8 0		2 tens	20

Add.

	4 tens	4 0		9 tens	9 0
	+5 tens	+5 0		−5 tens	−5 0
	tens			tens	

Subtract.

	1 ten	1 0		6 tens	6 0
	+5 tens	+5 0		−5 tens	−5 0
	tens			ten	

3 0	8 0	6 0	5 0	6 0	9 0
+4 0	+1 0	+3 0	−4 0	−2 0	−3 0

2 0	4 0	1 0	2 0	9 0	3 0
+3 0	+4 0	+7 0	−1 0	−7 0	−2 0

5 0	6 0	3 0	8 0	7 0	9 0
+2 0	+1 0	+3 0	−3 0	−4 0	−6 0

Perfect score: 26   My score: _____

Problem Solving

Solve each problem.

There are 90  .

40 are used.

How many are not used?

$$\begin{array}{r} 90 \\ -40 \\ \hline \end{array}$$

You have 20  .

You buy 30 more.

Now how many do you have?

$$\begin{array}{r} 20 \\ +30 \\ \hline \end{array}$$

Gina had 60 .

She spent 40 .

How many does she have left?

Ned found 10 .

Then he found 20 more.

Now how many does he have?

There were 80 .

60 ran away.

Then how many were there?

Perfect score: 5   My score: _____

74

Lesson 3 Addition (2 digits)

Join the pennies.
Add the ones.

Join the dimes.
Add the tens.

$$\begin{array}{r} 34 \\ +25 \\ \hline 9 \end{array}$$ → $$\begin{array}{r} 34 \\ +25 \\ \hline 59 \end{array}$$

Add.

$$\begin{array}{r} 47 \\ +\ 2 \\ \hline 49 \end{array}$$

— Add the ones.
— Add the tens.

$$\begin{array}{r} 52 \\ +44 \\ \hline \end{array}$$

$$\begin{array}{r} 84 \\ +10 \\ \hline \end{array}$$

$$\begin{array}{r} 26 \\ +13 \\ \hline \end{array}$$

$$\begin{array}{r} 11 \\ +14 \\ \hline \end{array}$$

$$\begin{array}{r} 31 \\ +12 \\ \hline \end{array}$$

$$\begin{array}{r} 12 \\ +\ 1 \\ \hline \end{array}$$

$$\begin{array}{r} 78 \\ +11 \\ \hline \end{array}$$

$$\begin{array}{r} 43 \\ +10 \\ \hline \end{array}$$

$$\begin{array}{r} 50 \\ +18 \\ \hline \end{array}$$

$$\begin{array}{r} 18 \\ +50 \\ \hline \end{array}$$

$$\begin{array}{r} 81 \\ +\ 5 \\ \hline \end{array}$$

$$\begin{array}{r} 75 \\ +23 \\ \hline \end{array}$$

$$\begin{array}{r} 54 \\ +42 \\ \hline \end{array}$$

$$\begin{array}{r} 43 \\ +16 \\ \hline \end{array}$$

$$\begin{array}{r} 22 \\ +26 \\ \hline \end{array}$$

$$\begin{array}{r} 43 \\ +\ 2 \\ \hline \end{array}$$

$$\begin{array}{r} 33 \\ +54 \\ \hline \end{array}$$

$$\begin{array}{r} 31 \\ +26 \\ \hline \end{array}$$

Perfect score: 19   My score: _____

Solve each problem.

There are 24 .

35 more are planted.

Now how many are there?

Al had 27  .

He bought 12 more.

Now how many does he have?

Ima has 54 .

Ida has 34 .

How many do they have in all?

You found 82 .

Then you find 7 more.

Now how many do you have?

---

20 are blue.

79 are white.

How many and are there in all?

Lesson 4   Addition (2 digits)

Add.

24	75	50	62	46
+13	+ 4	+27	+15	+23
37	79			

52	96	73	38	35
+34	+ 2	+16	+40	+21

10	14	12	33	13
+21	+ 5	+34	+53	+11

24	57	60	12	71
+21	+ 2	+33	+43	+26

16	28	51	40	63
+52	+ 1	+27	+45	+16

22	64	24	41	31
+67	+ 4	+72	+38	+56

Perfect score: 30   My score: _____

Problem Solving

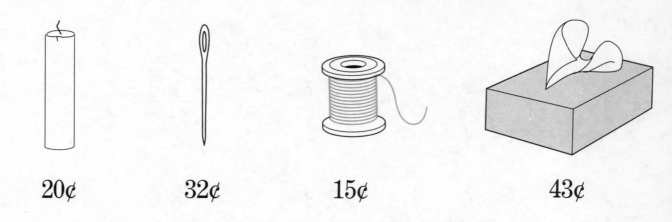

20¢   32¢   15¢   43¢

Solve each problem.

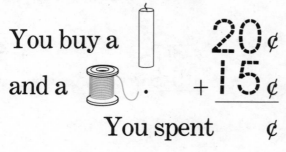
You buy a | and a | .

20¢
+ 15¢
You spent ____ ¢

You buy a | and a | .

15¢
+ 32¢
You spent ____ ¢

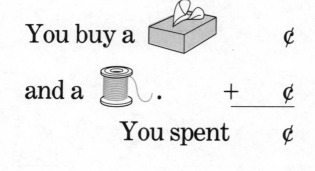
You buy a | ____ ¢
and a | . + ____ ¢
You spent ____ ¢

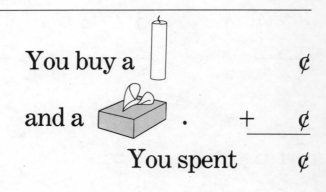
You buy a | ____ ¢
and a | . + ____ ¢
You spent ____ ¢

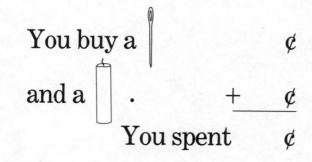
You buy a | ____ ¢
and a | . + ____ ¢
You spent ____ ¢

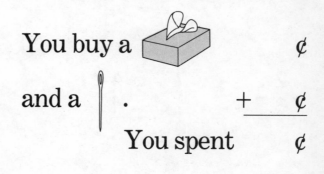
You buy a | ____ ¢
and a | . + ____ ¢
You spent ____ ¢

Perfect score: 6   My score: _____

Lesson 5　Subtraction (2 digits)

Take away 4 pennies.
Subtract the ones.

Take away 2 dimes.
Subtract the tens.

$$\begin{array}{r} 36 \\ -24 \\ \hline 2 \end{array}$$
⇒
$$\begin{array}{r} 36 \\ -24 \\ \hline 12 \end{array}$$

Subtract.

$$\begin{array}{r} 78 \\ -6 \\ \hline 72 \end{array}$$
— Subtract the ones.
— Subtract the tens.

$$\begin{array}{r} 69 \\ -47 \\ \hline \end{array}$$

$$\begin{array}{r} 28 \\ -15 \\ \hline \end{array}$$

$$\begin{array}{r} 45 \\ -32 \\ \hline \end{array}$$

$$\begin{array}{r} 59 \\ -45 \\ \hline \end{array}$$

$$\begin{array}{r} 98 \\ -43 \\ \hline \end{array}$$

$$\begin{array}{r} 17 \\ -5 \\ \hline \end{array}$$

$$\begin{array}{r} 57 \\ -43 \\ \hline \end{array}$$

$$\begin{array}{r} 48 \\ -34 \\ \hline \end{array}$$

$$\begin{array}{r} 58 \\ -17 \\ \hline \end{array}$$

$$\begin{array}{r} 85 \\ -25 \\ \hline \end{array}$$

$$\begin{array}{r} 87 \\ -7 \\ \hline \end{array}$$

$$\begin{array}{r} 96 \\ -80 \\ \hline \end{array}$$

$$\begin{array}{r} 66 \\ -51 \\ \hline \end{array}$$

$$\begin{array}{r} 94 \\ -41 \\ \hline \end{array}$$

$$\begin{array}{r} 39 \\ -22 \\ \hline \end{array}$$

$$\begin{array}{r} 33 \\ -2 \\ \hline \end{array}$$

$$\begin{array}{r} 65 \\ -22 \\ \hline \end{array}$$

$$\begin{array}{r} 78 \\ -65 \\ \hline \end{array}$$

Perfect score: 19　My score: _____

Problem Solving

Solve each problem.

There are 54 🌹 .

32 were picked.
How many are left?

$$\begin{array}{r} 54 \\ -\ 32 \\ \hline \end{array}$$

You have 48 ⬜ .

35 are blue.
The rest are white.
How many white ones are there?

A store has 99 🔨 .

The store sold 73.

How many 🔨 does the store have now?

Ilsa has 23 ✉ .

Neal has 12 ✉ .

How many more ✉ does Ilsa have than Neal?

To build a 🏠 you need 48 🔩 .

You have 28 🔩 .

How many more 🔩 do you need?

Perfect score: 5   My score: _____

80

Lesson 6 Subtraction (2 digits)

Subtract.

7 5 −3 4 **41**	6 7 − 4 **63**	3 0 −2 0	4 8 −3 0	5 5 −3 2
7 8 −6 7	5 6 − 3	9 8 −8 6	8 6 −1 5	9 8 −4 8
9 5 −3 1	8 4 − 2	6 5 −4 5	7 9 −4 8	8 4 −5 0
4 2 −1 0	3 9 − 6	8 9 −4 2	6 7 −2 1	6 6 −3 6
9 8 −7 3	7 2 − 2	4 3 −1 3	5 7 −3 2	6 9 −1 5
3 2 −1 1	9 7 − 5	7 8 −2 2	9 9 −1 6	8 7 −4 7

Perfect score: 30   My score: _____

Problem Solving

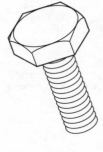

59¢   15¢   42¢   30¢

Solve each problem.

You have	6 2¢		You have	5 0¢
You buy a	−42¢		You buy a	−30¢
You have left	20¢		You have left	¢

You have	5 3¢		You have	9 9¢
You buy a	− ¢		You buy a	− ¢
You have left	¢		You have left	¢

You have	7 6¢		You have	4 5¢
You buy a	− ¢		You buy a	− ¢
You have left	¢		You have left	¢

Perfect score: 6   My score: _____

Lesson 7   Adding 3 Numbers

Add the ones.

Add the tens.

```
 12 ---> 5       60 <--- 12
 53 ---/           --- 53
+24 ---> +4     +20    +24
     9 <---          ---> 89
```

Add.

```
  4 5        3 2        3 5        4 7
  3 3        3 7        2 1        2 0
+ 1 0      + 2 0      + 1 1      + 2 2
  8 8        8 9
```

└ ── Add the ones.
└ ──── Add the tens.

```
  2 4        3 1        4 0        5 4        4 5
  2 4        2 3        1 3        1 0        3 3
+ 2 1      + 3 1      + 1 1      + 2 3      + 1 0
```

```
  6 1        3 0        3 6        3 1        4 4
  1 2        2 4        3 2        2 0        2 0
+ 2 4      + 1 5      + 3 1      + 2 4      + 3 4
```

Perfect score: 14   My score: _____

83

Problem Solving

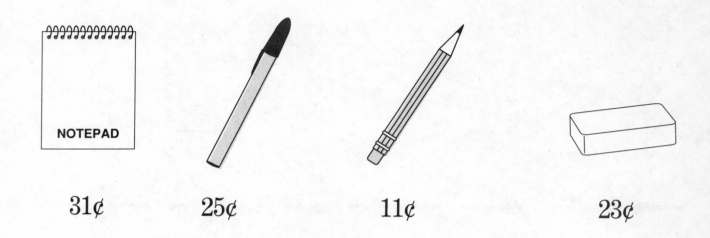

31¢   25¢   11¢   23¢

Solve each problem.

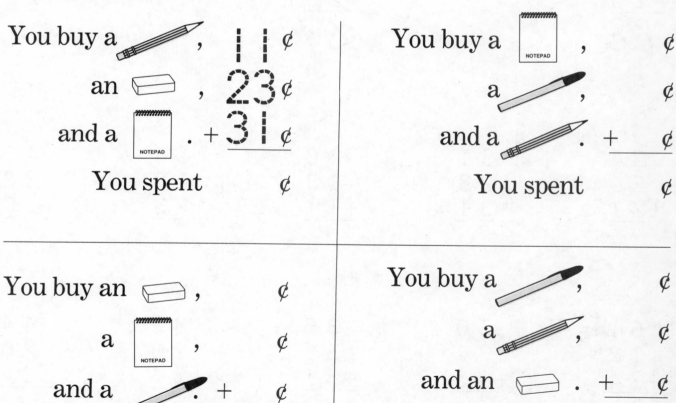

Lesson 8   Addition and Subtraction

Add or subtract.   Watch the + and −!

3 2 +3 4	5 7 −2 5	8 2 − 2	9 2 −6 1	4 2 +5 7
8 6 −5 2	1 5 +6 2	4 0 + 7	3 1 +1 5	7 3 −1 3
6 9 +3 0	3 4 −1 2	8 7 − 6	8 4 +1 4	4 0 +3 5
9 5 −2 5	8 6 −4 3	7 7 + 2	6 1 +1 7	5 9 −4 4
3 9 +6 0	6 8 −6 7	5 5 + 4	8 8 −8 3	9 6 −8 1

Perfect score: 25   My score: _____

Problem Solving

Solve each problem.

There are 43 white ⬭ .

There are 45 blue 🔵 .

How many more blue 🔵 than

white ⬭ are there?

$$\begin{array}{r} 45 \\ -\ 43 \\ \hline \end{array}$$

There are 19 🐦 .

30 more come.
How many are there now?

---

34 🥛 are on the table.

2 are broken.
How many are not broken?

You need 19 📎 .

You have 7 📎 .

How many more do you need?

You have 32 .

You get 57 more.
Now how many do you have?

Perfect score: 5   My score: _____

Lesson 9 Addition and Subtraction

Add or subtract.   Watch the + and −!

If you get 56, color that part.

2 2 +3 4 **56**	7 8 −2 4	5 9 − 3	7 5 −1 1	1 5 +4 1
9 6 −4 0	1 5 +6 2	5 0 + 6	6 1 +1 5	6 7 −1 1
6 9 −1 3	7 8 −2 2	5 7 − 1	8 4 +1 4	4 0 +1 6
9 7 −4 1	8 6 −3 2	5 4 + 2	6 1 +1 7	9 9 −4 3
3 1 +2 5	6 8 −6 7	5 2 + 4	8 8 −8 3	7 9 −2 3

Perfect score: 25   My score: _____

87

Chapter 7   Checkup

Add.

$$
\begin{array}{r} 3\,0 \\ +5\,0 \\ \hline \end{array}
\qquad
\begin{array}{r} 3\,4 \\ +\ 5 \\ \hline \end{array}
\qquad
\begin{array}{r} 6\,1 \\ +2\,4 \\ \hline \end{array}
\qquad
\begin{array}{r} 1\,8 \\ +3\,1 \\ \hline \end{array}
\qquad
\begin{array}{r} 5\,0 \\ +3\,6 \\ \hline \end{array}
$$

$$
\begin{array}{r} 4\,5 \\ +2\,1 \\ \hline \end{array}
\qquad
\begin{array}{r} 9\,2 \\ +\ 7 \\ \hline \end{array}
\qquad
\begin{array}{r} 7\,3 \\ +1\,3 \\ \hline \end{array}
\qquad
\begin{array}{r} 5\,4 \\ +2\,4 \\ \hline \end{array}
\qquad
\begin{array}{r} 8\,2 \\ +1\,7 \\ \hline \end{array}
$$

$$
\begin{array}{r} 3\,5 \\ +1\,2 \\ \hline \end{array}
\qquad
\begin{array}{r} 6\,0 \\ +\ 8 \\ \hline \end{array}
\qquad
\begin{array}{r} 3\,0 \\ 4\,0 \\ +1\,0 \\ \hline \end{array}
\qquad
\begin{array}{r} 5\,1 \\ 1\,6 \\ +1\,2 \\ \hline \end{array}
\qquad
\begin{array}{r} 2\,6 \\ 2\,1 \\ +1\,2 \\ \hline \end{array}
$$

Subtract.

$$
\begin{array}{r} 7\,0 \\ -4\,0 \\ \hline \end{array}
\qquad
\begin{array}{r} 8\,5 \\ -\ 2 \\ \hline \end{array}
\qquad
\begin{array}{r} 5\,4 \\ -3\,0 \\ \hline \end{array}
\qquad
\begin{array}{r} 9\,7 \\ -3\,5 \\ \hline \end{array}
\qquad
\begin{array}{r} 7\,4 \\ -5\,4 \\ \hline \end{array}
$$

$$
\begin{array}{r} 2\,8 \\ -1\,8 \\ \hline \end{array}
\qquad
\begin{array}{r} 7\,8 \\ -\ 4 \\ \hline \end{array}
\qquad
\begin{array}{r} 4\,6 \\ -2\,3 \\ \hline \end{array}
\qquad
\begin{array}{r} 8\,9 \\ -3\,3 \\ \hline \end{array}
\qquad
\begin{array}{r} 9\,3 \\ -6\,2 \\ \hline \end{array}
$$

Perfect score: 25   My score: _____

Add or subtract.

$$\begin{array}{r} 8 \\ +3 \\ \hline 11 \end{array}$$

$$\begin{array}{r} 3 \\ +8 \\ \hline \end{array}$$

$$\begin{array}{r} 11 \\ -\ 8 \\ \hline 3 \end{array}$$

$$\begin{array}{r} 11 \\ -\ 3 \\ \hline \end{array}$$

$$\begin{array}{r} 9 \\ +2 \\ \hline \end{array}$$

$$\begin{array}{r} 2 \\ +9 \\ \hline \end{array}$$

$$\begin{array}{r} 11 \\ -\ 9 \\ \hline \end{array}$$
$$\begin{array}{r} 11 \\ -\ 2 \\ \hline \end{array}$$

$$\begin{array}{r} 6 \\ +5 \\ \hline \end{array}$$

$$\begin{array}{r} 5 \\ +6 \\ \hline \end{array}$$

$$\begin{array}{r} 11 \\ -\ 6 \\ \hline \end{array}$$

$$\begin{array}{r} 11 \\ -\ 5 \\ \hline \end{array}$$

$$\begin{array}{r} 7 \\ +4 \\ \hline \end{array}$$

$$\begin{array}{r} 4 \\ +7 \\ \hline \end{array}$$

$$\begin{array}{r} 11 \\ -\ 7 \\ \hline \end{array}$$

$$\begin{array}{r} 11 \\ -\ 4 \\ \hline \end{array}$$

$$\begin{array}{r} 7 \\ +4 \\ \hline \end{array}$$
$$\begin{array}{r} 6 \\ +5 \\ \hline \end{array}$$
$$\begin{array}{r} 3 \\ +8 \\ \hline \end{array}$$

$$\begin{array}{r} 11 \\ -\ 6 \\ \hline \end{array}$$
$$\begin{array}{r} 11 \\ -\ 9 \\ \hline \end{array}$$
$$\begin{array}{r} 11 \\ -\ 7 \\ \hline \end{array}$$

$$\begin{array}{r} 11 \\ +\ 0 \\ \hline \end{array}$$
$$\begin{array}{r} 9 \\ +2 \\ \hline \end{array}$$
$$\begin{array}{r} 5 \\ +6 \\ \hline \end{array}$$

$$\begin{array}{r} 11 \\ -\ 2 \\ \hline \end{array}$$
$$\begin{array}{r} 11 \\ -\ 0 \\ \hline \end{array}$$
$$\begin{array}{r} 11 \\ -\ 8 \\ \hline \end{array}$$

Perfect score: 28   My score: _____

Problem Solving

Solve each problem.

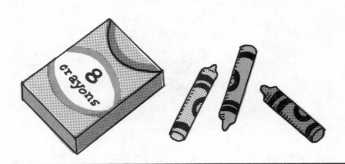

$$8$$ crayons in a box

$$+\ 3$$ more crayons

crayons in all

$+$ birds on a wire

birds coming

birds in all

blue hats

$+$ black hats

hats in all

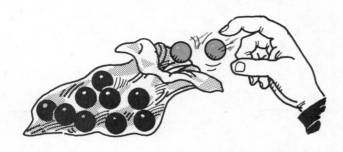

marbles in a bag

$+$ marbles are put in

marbles in all

ants on a hill

$+$ ants coming

ants in all

Lesson 2   Facts for 12

Add or subtract.

$$\begin{array}{r} 8 \\ +4 \\ \hline 12 \end{array}$$

$$\begin{array}{r} 4 \\ +8 \\ \hline \end{array}$$

$$\begin{array}{r} 1\,2 \\ -\ 8 \\ \hline 4 \end{array}$$

$$\begin{array}{r} 1\,2 \\ -\ 4 \\ \hline \end{array}$$

$$\begin{array}{r} 9 \\ +3 \\ \hline \end{array}$$

$$\begin{array}{r} 3 \\ +9 \\ \hline \end{array}$$

$$\begin{array}{r} 1\,2 \\ -\ 9 \\ \hline \end{array}$$

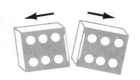

$$\begin{array}{r} 1\,2 \\ -\ 3 \\ \hline \end{array}$$

$$\begin{array}{r} 7 \\ +5 \\ \hline \end{array}$$

$$\begin{array}{r} 5 \\ +7 \\ \hline \end{array}$$

$$\begin{array}{r} 1\,2 \\ -\ 7 \\ \hline \end{array}$$

$$\begin{array}{r} 1\,2 \\ -\ 5 \\ \hline \end{array}$$

$$\begin{array}{r} 6 \\ +6 \\ \hline \end{array}$$

$$\begin{array}{r} 1\,2 \\ -\ 6 \\ \hline \end{array}$$

$$\begin{array}{r} 9 \\ +3 \\ \hline \end{array}$$
$$\begin{array}{r} 5 \\ +7 \\ \hline \end{array}$$
$$\begin{array}{r} 1\,2 \\ +\ 0 \\ \hline \end{array}$$
$$\begin{array}{r} 1\,2 \\ -\ 6 \\ \hline \end{array}$$
$$\begin{array}{r} 1\,2 \\ -\ 0 \\ \hline \end{array}$$
$$\begin{array}{r} 1\,2 \\ -\ 8 \\ \hline \end{array}$$

$$\begin{array}{r} 6 \\ +6 \\ \hline \end{array}$$
$$\begin{array}{r} 4 \\ +8 \\ \hline \end{array}$$
$$\begin{array}{r} 7 \\ +5 \\ \hline \end{array}$$
$$\begin{array}{r} 1\,2 \\ -\ 5 \\ \hline \end{array}$$
$$\begin{array}{r} 1\,2 \\ -\ 9 \\ \hline \end{array}$$
$$\begin{array}{r} 1\,2 \\ -\ 4 \\ \hline \end{array}$$

Perfect score: 26   My score: _____

Problem Solving

Solve each problem.

$\begin{array}{r} 12 \\ - 4 \\ \hline \end{array}$ birds in all

birds flying away

birds stay

$\begin{array}{r} \\ - \\ \hline \end{array}$ cars in all

cars leaving

cars stay

$\begin{array}{r} \\ - \\ \hline \end{array}$ flowers in all

blue flowers

white flowers

$\begin{array}{r} \\ - \\ \hline \end{array}$ buttons in all

black buttons

blue buttons

$\begin{array}{r} \\ - \\ \hline \end{array}$ berries in all

berries falling

berries not falling

Perfect score: 5   My score: _____

Lesson 3 Facts Through 12

NAME _____

Add.

8 +4 **12**	7 +4	6 +6	3 +9	9 +2	6 +5
5 +5	7 +5	9 +1	4 +8	5 +7	3 +8
4 +6	2 +9	8 +3	4 +7	9 +3	5 +6

Subtract.

12 − 8 **4**	11 − 9	12 − 5	11 − 4	12 − 6	11 − 0
12 − 3	12 − 7	10 − 3	11 − 8	10 − 6	11 − 5
12 − 0	11 − 2	10 − 8	12 − 4	11 − 7	12 − 9

Perfect score: 36   My score: _____

Problem Solving

Solve each problem.

$$+\ \underline{}$$

_____ books on top shelf
_____ books on bottom shelf
_____ books in all

$$-\ \underline{}$$

_____ cars parked
_____ cars going
_____ more cars are parked

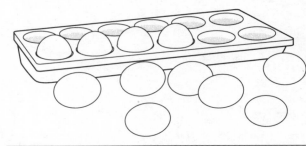

$$+\ \underline{}$$

_____ eggs in the carton
_____ eggs on the table
_____ eggs in all

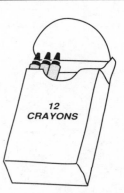

$$-\ \underline{}$$

_____ crayons that can be in the box
_____ crayons in the box
_____ crayons needed to fill the box

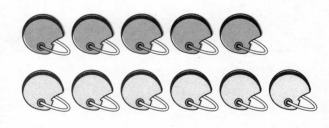

$$+\ \underline{}$$

_____ blue football helmets
_____ gray football helmets
_____ helmets in all

Perfect score: 5   My score: _____

94

Lesson 4 Facts for 13

Add or subtract.

7 +6 **13**		6 +7	1 3 − 7 **6**		1 3 − 6
8 +5		5 +8	1 3 − 8		1 3 − 5
9 +4		4 +9	1 3 − 9		1 3 − 4

5 +8	9 +4	7 +6	1 3 − 5	1 3 − 7	1 3 − 9
6 +7	8 +5	4 +9	1 3 − 4	1 3 − 8	1 3 − 6

Perfect score: 24   My score: _____

Lesson 5 Facts for 14

Add or subtract.

9 +5 **14**	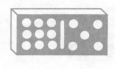	5 +9	14 − 9 **5**		14 − 5
8 +6		6 +8	14 − 8		14 − 6
7 +7			14 − 7	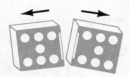	

8	7	6	14	12	14
+6	+7	+6	− 8	− 7	− 5

9	5	7	14	13	14
+4	+9	+4	− 7	− 8	− 6

9	6	6	11	14	12
+5	+7	+8	− 8	− 9	− 4

Lesson 6 Facts Through 14

Add.

9 +4 **13**	7 +7	6 +5	8 +4	5 +9	4 +7
5 +6	9 +5	5 +7	8 +5	7 +6	6 +8
3 +8	7 +5	8 +6	5 +8	4 +9	6 +6

Subtract.

12 − 5 **7**	13 − 7	14 − 5	11 − 3	14 − 7	13 − 6
13 − 8	12 − 9	14 − 6	11 − 5	14 − 9	12 − 6
11 − 7	11 − 9	13 − 4	12 − 8	13 − 9	14 − 8

Perfect score: 36   My score: _____

Problem Solving

Solve each problem.

$$\begin{array}{r} 8 \\ +\ 6 \\ \hline \end{array}$$

trucks in a box

other trucks

trucks in all

$$\begin{array}{r} \\ -\ \\ \hline \end{array}$$

turtles in all

turtles going away

turtles stay

$$\begin{array}{r} \\ +\ \\ \hline \end{array}$$

candles on the cake

other candles

candles in all

$$\begin{array}{r} \\ +\ \\ \hline \end{array}$$

marbles in a bag

more marbles

marbles in all

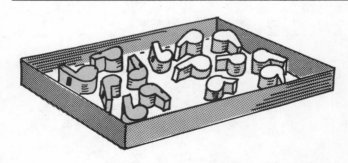

$$\begin{array}{r} \\ -\ \\ \hline \end{array}$$

whistles in the box

white whistles

blue whistles

Perfect score: 5   My score: _____

98

Lesson 7 Facts for 15

Add or subtract.

```
    8          7         1 5        1 5
  +7         +8         - 7        - 8
  15                      8
```

```
    9          6         1 5        1 5
  +6         +9         - 6        - 9
```

```
    6          7          8    │    1 4        1 5        1 3
  +9         +8         +6    │    - 9        - 8        - 7
```

```
    6          9          8    │    1 5        1 4        1 5
  +8         +5         +7    │    - 9        - 6        - 7
```

```
    8          9          7    │    1 3        1 5        1 4
  +5         +6         +7    │    - 8        - 6        - 5
```

Perfect score: 26   My score: _____

Lesson 8 Facts for 16

Add or subtract.

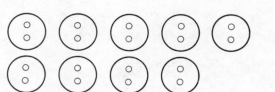

9	7	1 6	1 6
+7	+9	− 7	− 9
16		9	

8	1 6
+8	− 8

8	9	7	1 6	1 5	1 4
+7	+7	+8	− 9	− 7	− 5

8	5	7	1 4	1 5	1 6
+8	+9	+7	− 9	− 6	− 8

7	6	9	1 4	1 6	1 5
+9	+8	+6	− 8	− 7	− 9

Perfect score: 24   My score: _____

Lesson 9 Facts Through 16

Add.

7 +8 **15**	6 +6	5 +9	8 +4	7 +7	6 +9
8 +8	9 +4	7 +6	8 +6	7 +9	8 +3
5 +6	8 +7	9 +7	8 +5	6 +8	9 +6

Subtract.

14 −7 **7**	15 −6	16 −7	13 −8	14 −5	12 −9
12 −6	14 −6	11 −9	16 −8	11 −3	15 −9
15 −7	13 −9	16 −9	14 −9	15 −8	14 −8

Perfect score: 36   My score: _____

Problem Solving

Solve each problem.

$\begin{array}{r} 16 \\ -\ 8 \\ \hline \end{array}$ balloons in all

balloons broken

balloons not broken

_____ cartons in all

$-$ _____ cartons open

_____ cartons closed

_____ books in a box

$+$ _____ books in a pile

_____ books in all

_____ glasses in all

$-$ _____ glasses filled

_____ glasses empty

_____ ¢ for a yo-yo

$+$ _____ ¢ for a top

_____ ¢ for both

Perfect score: 5   My score: _____

102

Lesson 10   Facts Through 18

Add or subtract.

$$\begin{array}{r} 9 \\ +8 \\ \hline 17 \end{array} \qquad \begin{array}{r} 8 \\ +9 \\ \hline \end{array} \qquad \begin{array}{r} 17 \\ -8 \\ \hline 9 \end{array} \qquad \begin{array}{r} 17 \\ -9 \\ \hline \end{array}$$

$$\begin{array}{r} 9 \\ +9 \\ \hline \end{array} \qquad\qquad\qquad \begin{array}{r} 18 \\ -9 \\ \hline \end{array}$$

$$\begin{array}{r} 6 \\ +8 \\ \hline \end{array} \qquad \begin{array}{r} 8 \\ +8 \\ \hline \end{array} \qquad \begin{array}{r} 8 \\ +9 \\ \hline \end{array} \qquad \begin{array}{r} 17 \\ -8 \\ \hline \end{array} \qquad \begin{array}{r} 15 \\ -7 \\ \hline \end{array} \qquad \begin{array}{r} 16 \\ -9 \\ \hline \end{array}$$

$$\begin{array}{r} 7 \\ +9 \\ \hline \end{array} \qquad \begin{array}{r} 8 \\ +7 \\ \hline \end{array} \qquad \begin{array}{r} 9 \\ +6 \\ \hline \end{array} \qquad \begin{array}{r} 14 \\ -7 \\ \hline \end{array} \qquad \begin{array}{r} 18 \\ -9 \\ \hline \end{array} \qquad \begin{array}{r} 16 \\ -8 \\ \hline \end{array}$$

$$\begin{array}{r} 9 \\ +8 \\ \hline \end{array} \qquad \begin{array}{r} 8 \\ +8 \\ \hline \end{array} \qquad \begin{array}{r} 9 \\ +9 \\ \hline \end{array} \qquad \begin{array}{r} 15 \\ -6 \\ \hline \end{array} \qquad \begin{array}{r} 17 \\ -9 \\ \hline \end{array} \qquad \begin{array}{r} 16 \\ -7 \\ \hline \end{array}$$

Perfect score: 24   My score: _____

Problem Solving

Solve each problem.

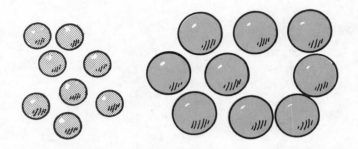

$$
\begin{array}{r}
17 \\
-\ 8 \\
\hline

\end{array}
$$

balls in all

small balls

large balls

$$
\begin{array}{r}
 \\
+\ \\
\hline

\end{array}
$$

jars on top shelf

jars on bottom shelf

jars in all

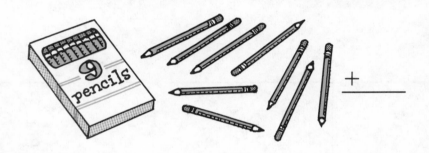

$$
\begin{array}{r}
 \\
+\ \\
\hline

\end{array}
$$

pencils in a box

more pencils

pencils in all

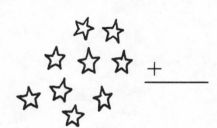

$$
\begin{array}{r}
 \\
+\ \\
\hline

\end{array}
$$

big stars

small stars

stars in all

$$
\begin{array}{r}
 \\
-\ \\
\hline

\end{array}
$$

bees in all

bees go away

bees stay

Perfect score: 5   My score: _____

104

NAME _____

Lesson 11 Addition Facts Through 18
Add.

5 +7 **12**	7 +5	2 +9	9 +2	5 +8	8 +5
6 +4	4 +6	9 +4	4 +9	6 +8	8 +6
7 +8	8 +7	4 +8	8 +4	9 +6	6 +9
7 +7	5 +6	6 +5	5 +9	9 +5	8 +8
5 +5	7 +6	6 +7	9 +8	8 +9	6 +6
7 +9	9 +7	4 +8	8 +3	7 +3	9 +9

Perfect score: 36   My score: _____

105

Addition Facts Through 18

Ring each name for the number in the ⬤.

4 + 8   **11**   (9 + 2)

(5 + 6)   6 + 6

(4 + 7)   (8 + 3)

---

3 + 8   **12**   3 + 9

6 + 6   6 + 7   8 + 4

7 + 5   5 + 8   5 + 6

---

8 + 5   **13**   7 + 6

6 + 8   9 + 5

9 + 4   6 + 7   4 + 8

---

8 + 6   **14**   9 + 5

6 + 7   7 + 7

6 + 8   8 + 8

---

7 + 7   **15**   9 + 6

8 + 7   6 + 9

5 + 9   7 + 8

---

5 + 7   **16**   6 + 9

8 + 7   9 + 7

7 + 9   8 + 8

---

8 + 9   **17**   9 + 9

8 + 8   6 + 9

8 + 7   9 + 8

---

5 + 8   **18**   4 + 6

9 + 9   8 + 7

6 + 9

Perfect score: 26   My score: _____

Lesson 12 Subtraction Facts Through 18

Subtract.

1 5 − 7 **8**	1 5 − 8	1 3 − 9	1 3 − 4	1 2 − 8	1 2 − 4
1 4 − 6	1 4 − 8	1 1 − 7	1 1 − 4	1 0 − 7	1 0 − 3
1 5 − 6	1 5 − 9	1 4 − 9	1 4 − 5	1 7 − 8	1 7 − 9
1 6 − 8	1 6 − 7	1 6 − 9	1 3 − 5	1 3 − 8	1 4 − 7
1 2 − 6	1 1 − 3	1 1 − 8	1 3 − 7	1 3 − 6	1 0 − 5
1 0 − 8	1 0 − 2	1 2 − 5	1 2 − 7	1 8 − 9	1 5 − 7

Perfect score: 36   My score: _____

How many subtraction facts do you know?

0	1	2	3	4	5	6	7	8	9
R	I	U	Y	E	K	O	V	W	N

Subtract. Write the letter for each answer.

$$
\begin{array}{ccccccc}
11 & 15 & 10 & 14 & 16 & 14 & 15 \\
-\ 8 & -\ 9 & -\ 8 & -\ 9 & -\ 7 & -\ 8 & -\ 7 \\
\end{array}
$$

3

Y

$$
\begin{array}{cccccccc}
7 & 9 & 8 & 9 & 10 & 11 & 11 & 13 \\
-3 & -2 & -4 & -9 & -\ 7 & -\ 5 & -\ 2 & -\ 9 \\
\end{array}
$$

$$
\begin{array}{cccccc}
12 & 13 & 11 & 16 & 10 & 18 \\
-\ 9 & -\ 7 & -\ 9 & -\ 8 & -\ 9 & -\ 9 \\
\end{array}
$$

Perfect score: 42   My score: _____

Chapter 8   Checkup

Add.

9 +8	5 +7	8 +6	7 +5	4 +9	5 +6
7 +6	8 +8	5 +9	9 +9	7 +8	6 +6
4 +7	9 +2	7 +7	8 +4	9 +6	7 +9

Subtract.

13 − 6	14 − 7	15 − 6	11 − 3	12 − 8	16 − 9
13 − 8	12 − 9	11 − 5	17 − 8	18 − 9	15 − 7
14 − 8	11 − 7	12 − 6	14 − 5	11 − 9	17 − 9

Turn the page.

Problem Solving

Solve each problem.

_____ open boxes

+ _____ closed boxes

_____ boxes in all

 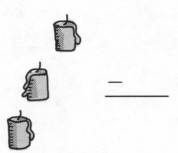

_____ candles in all

− _____ blue candles

_____ white candles

_____ jars in a box

+ _____ other jars

_____ jars in all

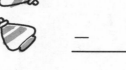

_____ tops in all

− _____ tops not spinning

_____ tops spinning

Checkup—Chapters 1–4

Ring the numeral.

| 0 | 1 | 2 | 3 |  4 | 5 | 6 | 7 |  7 | 8 | 9 | 10 |

     2¢   5¢   6¢

   1¢   5¢   10¢

    4¢   8¢   9¢

Add.

$$\begin{array}{r} 2 \\ +1 \\ \hline \end{array} \qquad \begin{array}{r} 4 \\ +5 \\ \hline \end{array} \qquad \begin{array}{r} 3 \\ +2 \\ \hline \end{array} \qquad \begin{array}{r} 6 \\ +1 \\ \hline \end{array} \qquad \begin{array}{r} 7 \\ +3 \\ \hline \end{array} \qquad \begin{array}{r} 5 \\ +0 \\ \hline \end{array}$$

$$\begin{array}{r} 5 \\ +5 \\ \hline \end{array} \qquad \begin{array}{r} 3 \\ +6 \\ \hline \end{array} \qquad \begin{array}{r} 4 \\ +3 \\ \hline \end{array} \qquad \begin{array}{r} 3 \\ +1 \\ \hline \end{array} \qquad \begin{array}{r} 2 \\ +6 \\ \hline \end{array} \qquad \begin{array}{r} 3 \\ +3 \\ \hline \end{array}$$

Subtract.

$$\begin{array}{r} 2 \\ -1 \\ \hline \end{array} \qquad \begin{array}{r} 6 \\ -4 \\ \hline \end{array} \qquad \begin{array}{r} 8 \\ -3 \\ \hline \end{array} \qquad \begin{array}{r} 4 \\ -2 \\ \hline \end{array} \qquad \begin{array}{r} 10 \\ -\ 2 \\ \hline \end{array} \qquad \begin{array}{r} 7 \\ -0 \\ \hline \end{array}$$

$$\begin{array}{r} 9 \\ -7 \\ \hline \end{array} \qquad \begin{array}{r} 7 \\ -5 \\ \hline \end{array} \qquad \begin{array}{r} 10 \\ -\ 4 \\ \hline \end{array} \qquad \begin{array}{r} 9 \\ -9 \\ \hline \end{array} \qquad \begin{array}{r} 10 \\ -\ 9 \\ \hline \end{array} \qquad \begin{array}{r} 5 \\ -2 \\ \hline \end{array}$$

Turn the page.

Checkup Chs. 1–4

Add or subtract. Watch the + and − signs!

4	6	4	1 0	1	8
+6	−1	+4	− 5	+8	−7

Solve each problem.

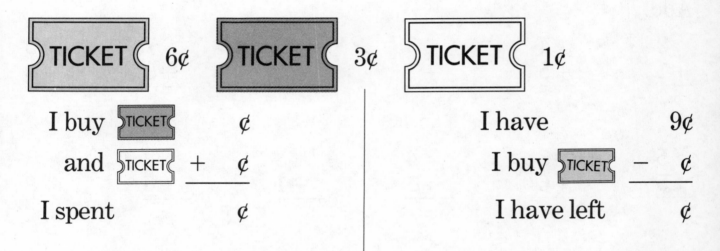

I buy [TICKET]   ___ ¢
and [TICKET] + ___ ¢
I spent   ___ ¢

I have   9¢
I buy [TICKET] − ___ ¢
I have left   ___ ¢

Matt has 7 .

He gave 2 away.

How many does he have now?

There are 6 blue   .

There are 3 white   .

How many are there in all?

Final Checkup

Tell how many cents.

_____ ¢

_____ ¢

_____ ¢

Name the numbers in order.

56, 57, 58, _____, _____, _____, _____

Write the time for each clock.

_____:_____

_____:_____

_____:_____

Final
Checkup

How long is each object?

_____ centimeters

_____ centimeters

_____ inches

_____ inches

Turn the page.

Add.

3	1	6	7	6
+1	+8	+4	+1	+2

5	8	4	0	3
+4	+2	+4	+7	+6

2 0	7 1	2 1	4 2	1 2
+1 4	+ 3	+2 5	+1 5	+6 7

Subtract.

5	7	3	4	6
−3	−1	−2	−3	−0

1 0	8	9	5	1 0
− 4	−5	−7	−1	− 5

6 8	7 2	3 9	8 4	5 7
−4 8	−5 0	− 4	−4 1	−5 2

Turn the page.

Final Checkup (Continued)

Add or subtract. Watch the + and − signs.

1 0 − 2	5 +5	7 +2	7 −3	1 0 − 7

5 1 +2 7	6 9 −1 0	4 3 + 2	8 7 −1 7	7 6 −6 2

Add.

3 +8	7 +7	8 +4	9 +9	8 +8

8 +7	4 +9	7 +6	6 +8	8 +9

Subtract.

1 2 − 6	1 4 − 7	1 1 − 8	1 5 − 9	1 7 − 8

1 3 − 9	1 5 − 8	1 6 − 7	1 4 − 6	1 8 − 9

Turn the page.

Solve each problem.

Jane has 2 ⚾ .

Bob has 6 ⚾ .   + ___

How many do they have in all?

---

9 🐦 were on the fence.

8 flew away.   − ___

How many are still on the fence?

You had 38¢.   ¢

You spent 23¢.   − ___ ¢

How much do you have left?   ¢

Arleta mailed 47 📮 .

Then she mailed 31 more.   + ___

How many 📮 did she mail in all?

+ ___   large balls

          small balls

          balls in all

− ___   cars in all

          black cars

          white cars

Perfect score: 80   My score: _____

116

Answers
Math - Grade 1
(Answers for Chapter Checkups are given on page 123.)

Page 1

0 1 (2) 3	0 (1) 2 3
0 1 2 (3)	0 1 (2) 3
0 1 2 (3)	0 (1) 2 3

Page 2

4 (5) 6 7	4 5 6 (7)
4 5 (6) 7	4 (5) 6 7
(4) 5 6 7	4 5 6 (7)

Page 3

8 9 (10)	(8) 9 10
8 9 (10)	8 (9) 10
(8) 9 10	8 9 (10)

Page 4

0
1
2
3
4
5
6
7
8
9
10

Page 5

7	4
6	10
8	2
9	3

Page 6

Page 7

1	2	3	4	5
6	7	8	9	10
10	9	8	7	6
5	4	3	2	1
1	2	3	4	5
6	7	8	9	10

Page 8

0	zero	4	four
1	one	5	five
2	two	6	six
3	three	7	seven

Page 9

| a crown | a frog |
| a butterfly | a stop sign |

Page 11

2	2		3	3
			3	3
2	2		3	3
2	2		3	3
0	0		1	1
			1	1

Page 12

5	5		5	5
5	5		5	5
			4	4
4	4		4	4
5	5		4	4
5	5		4	4

Page 13

	2			1
2			1	
	1			1
1			1	
	3			0
3			0	
	0			0
0			0	

Page 14

	4			1
4			1	
	1			0
1			0	
	3			2
3			2	
	2			3
2			3	

Page 15

3 3 1 2	4 4 3 1
5 5 3 2	5 5 1 4
2 1	4 2
2 2 0 2	5 5 0 5

Page 16

5¢	2¢
1¢	3¢
4¢	5¢
5¢	3¢

Page 17

1¢ +3¢ = 4¢	4¢ +1¢ = 5¢
2¢ +1¢ = 3¢	3¢ +2¢ = 5¢
5¢ −3¢ = 2¢	5¢ −1¢ = 4¢

Page 19

6 6	6 6
6 6	6 6
6 6	6 6
6 6	6 6
6 4 6	6 4 5

Page 20

	5			1
5			1	
	2			4
2			4	
	3			6
3			6	
3 0 5			2 4 1	

Page 21

7 7	7 7
7 7	7 7
7 7	7 7
7 7	7 7
7 6 7	7 7 6

Page 22

	1			6
1			6	
	4			3
4			3	
	0			7
0			7	
	5			2
5			2	

Page 23

8 8	8 8
8 8	8 8
8 8	8 8
8 8	8 8
6 8 8	8 7 8

117

Page 24

	1		7	7
1			7	
	6			2
6			2	
	4			0
4			0	
	5			3
5			3	

Page 25

8	7	6	8	8	6
7	6	8	6	7	7
8	8	7	6	8	8
5	1	4	4	4	0
3	7	7	1	2	2
0	3	6	6	5	5

Page 26

6	7	2	8	1
+2	−4	+3	−5	+5
8	3	5	3	6

Page 27

7	5	7	4	7	5
2	6	6	6	8	2
7	6	7	1	7	6
0	6	7	6	8	4
6	3	3	7	6	8
1	8	4	8	8	0

Page 28

8	4	7	6	7
−7	+3	+1	−4	−7
1	7	8	2	0

Page 29

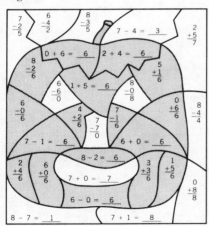

7 − 4 = 3
0 + 6 = 6   2 + 4 = 6
1 + 5 = 6
7 − 1 = 6   6 + 0 = 6
8 − 2 = 6
7 + 0 = 7
6 − 0 = 6
8 − 7 = 1   7 + 1 = 8

Page 31

9			9	
9			9	
9	9		9	9
9	9		9	9
9	9		9	9
9	9	9	9	9	8

Page 32

	3			6
3			6	
	9			0
9			0	
	4			5
4			5	
	1			8
1			8	
	7			2
7			2	

Page 33

	10			10
10			10	
10	10	10	10	10	10
10			10	
10	10	10	10	10	10
10	8	10	10	10	9

Page 34

	9			1
9			1	
3			6	
7	3	7	4	6	4
2			10		10
8	2	8			
3	9	5	0	8	4

Page 35

10	9	8	9	10	5
9	8	9	7	5	10
9	4	9	8	10	9
5	10	8	10	7	9
10	9	7	7	9	7
8	8	10	10	8	6

Page 36

5	3	9	6	8
+4	+7	+1	+3	+2
9	10	10	9	10

Page 37

5	1	5	2	3	1
6	3	3	7	9	4
2	8	2	5	4	0
9	7	2	1	8	2
1	3	10	2	4	6
4	2	7	7	0	3

Page 38

10	10	9	9	10
−4	−2	−6	−5	−5
6	8	3	4	5

Page 39

7	4	8	5	10	1
9	8	1	9	9	8
9	10	7	5	9	7
0	9	9	2	9	10
8	6	10	2	9	3
9	1	8	7	5	10

Page 40

9	7	5	10	9
−4	+2	+5	−6	−8
5	9	10	4	1

Page 41

10	6
6	8
10	5
10	9

Page 42

9¢	8¢	10¢	10¢
−5¢	−6¢	−8¢	−5¢
4¢	2¢	2¢	5¢

Page 43

	3¢		4¢
	+4¢		+6¢
	7¢		10¢
	10¢		9¢
	−6¢		−3¢
	4¢		6¢
	8¢		10¢
	−5¢		−4¢
	3¢		6¢

Page 45

1 ten 2 ones = 12
1 ten 3 ones = 13
1 ten 4 ones = 14
1 ten 5 ones = 15
1 ten 6 ones = 16
1 ten 7 ones = 17
1 ten 8 ones = 18
1 ten 9 ones = 19

Page 46

2 tens 2 ones = 22
2 tens 3 ones = 23
2 tens 4 ones = 24
2 tens 5 ones = 25
2 tens 6 ones = 26
2 tens 7 ones = 27
2 tens 8 ones = 28
2 tens 9 ones = 29

Page 47

2	3	23	2	0	20
1	5	15	2	6	26
2	2	22	1	7	17
1	3	13	2	4	24

Page 48

3 tens = 30
4 tens = 40
5 tens = 50
6 tens = 60
7 tens = 70
8 tens = 80
9 tens = 90

Page 49

3	2	32	3	4	34
3	9	39	4	0	40
		37			41
		49			35
		43			42
		33			44
		46			38

Page 50

0	1	2	3	4	5	6	7	8	9
10	11	12	13	14	15	16	17	18	19
20	21	22	23	24	25	26	27	28	29
30	31	32	33	34	35	36	37	38	39
40	41	42	43	44	45	46	47	48	49

a cat and a dog

Page 51

50	60
51	61
52	62
53	63
54	64
55	65
56	66
57	67
58	68
59	69

Page 52

74	88
91	79
78	87
98	89
85	92
99	73
70	96

Page 53

58¢	93¢
60¢	84¢
72¢	55¢
69¢	96¢

Page 54

50	51	52	53	54	55	56	57	58	59
60	61	62	63	64	65	66	67	68	69
70	71	72	73	74	75	76	77	78	79
80	81	82	83	84	85	86	87	88	89
90	91	92	93	94	95	96	97	98	99

an elephant

Page 55

26　~~31~~　(31)　|　~~36~~　(71)　68　|　~~40~~　70　(90)

(32)　~~31~~　30　|　85　~~66~~　(95)　|　(64)　46　~~48~~

~~34~~　(89)　87　|　(91)　57　~~60~~　|　78　(94)　~~46~~

18	37	93
63	30	89
69	54	50
33	21	68

Page 57

1; 1　　2; 2　　3; 3
4; 4:00　　5; 5:00　　6; 6:00
7; 7:00　　8; 8:00　　9; 9:00

Page 58

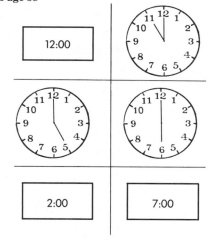

12:00

2:00　　7:00

Page 59

two thirty 2:30	three thirty 3:30	four thirty 4:30
eleven thirty 11:30	twelve thirty 12:30	five thirty 5:30
six thirty 6:30	ten thirty 10:30	eight thirty 8:30

Page 60

6:00

5:30　　7:30

Page 61

Friday　7　Friday　Tuesday　5
31　Wednesday　5　Friday　4

Page 62

November
February
January
December
31
Saturday
Answers will vary.
Have your teacher check your
answer.
February

Page 63

snowy　　sunny
rainy　　stormy
cloudy　　rainy
4　　2　　3　　8　　14

Page 64

Answers may vary. Have your
teacher check your work.

Page 65

12 centimeters
3 centimeters
6 centimeters
5 centimeters　　9 centimeters

Page 66

12 centimeters
4 centimeters　　8 centimeters
14 centimeters
6 centimeters
17 centimeters
3 centimeters

Page 67

2 inches　　3 inches
6 inches
1 inch　　2 inches

Page 68

2 inches
4 inches　　7 inches
4 inches
3 inches
1 inch　　6 inches

Page 69

Answers will vary. Have your teacher
check your work.

Page 71

7	8	10	4	9	5
9	4	2	10	7	9
3	10	10	8	8	10
7	0	3	7	2	7
1	3	1	2	1	7
2	3	4	2	1	3

Page 72

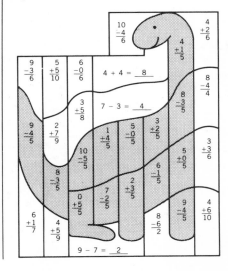

Page 102

16	15	8	16	7
-8	-7	$+7$	-7	$+9$
8	8	15	9	16

Page 103

17	17	9	8

18		9	

14	16	17	9	8	7
16	15	15	7	9	8
17	16	18	9	8	9

Page 104

17	9	9	8	18
-8	$+8$	$+9$	$+9$	-9
9	17	18	17	9

Page 105

12	12	11	11	13	13
10	10	13	13	14	14
15	15	12	12	15	15
14	11	11	14	14	16
10	13	13	17	17	12
16	16	12	11	10	18

Page 106

$5+6$	$9+2$	$6+6$	$3+9$
$4+7$	$8+3$	$7+5$	$8+4$
$8+5$	$7+6$	$8+6$	$9+5$
$9+4$	$6+7$	$6+8$	$7+7$
$8+7$	$9+6$		$9+7$
$6+9$	$7+8$	$7+9$	$8+8$
$8+9$	$9+8$	$9+9$	

Page 107

8	7	4	9	4	8
8	6	4	7	3	7
9	6	5	9	9	8
8	9	7	8	5	7
6	8	3	6	7	5
2	8	7	5	9	8

Page 108

3 6 2   5 9 6 8
Y O U   K N O W

4 7 4 0 3   6 9 4
E V E R Y   O N E

3 6 2   8 1 9
Y O U   W I N

Answers for Checkups for Grade 1

Page 10

5	7	1
9	0	6

XXX X	XX	X X
XXX	XX	X X
XXXXX X	X	XXXX
XXXXX	X	XXXX

Page 18

4	2	0	3	5	1
3	4	3	1	5	5
4	4	5	2	5	5
1	3	5	1	1	0
4	4	0	2	3	3
2	1	2	2	0	0

Page 30

8	6	7	7	8
6	8	6	7	8
2	5	2	3	8
7	2	4	6	5
6	5	3	7	1
0	7	4	7	8

Page 44

8	9	10	10	10
9	9	10	9	9
6	7	3	7	9
8	4	1	2	5
8	2	9	9	0
8	10	4	10	10

Page 56

14	60
37	99
28	45
83	54
70	31
92	66

16	17	18	19	20	21	22	23	24
42	43	44	45	46	47	48	49	50
79	80	81	82	83	84	85	86	87

Page 70

seven thirty   5:30   1:30
2 centimeters   8 centimeters
4 inches
1 inch   2 inches

Page 88

80	39	85	49	86
66	99	86	78	99
47	68	80	79	59
30	83	24	62	20
10	74	23	56	31

Page 109

17	12	14	12	13	11
13	16	14	18	15	12
11	11	14	12	15	16
7	7	9	8	4	7
5	3	6	9	9	8
6	4	6	9	2	8

Page 110

6	12	8	11
+8	−3	+7	−3
14	9	15	8

Page 111

2	5	10		
2¢	10¢	8¢		
3	9	5	7	10	5
10	9	7	4	8	6
1	2	5	2	8	7
2	2	6	0	1	3

Page 112

10	5	8	5	9	1

3¢	9¢
+1¢	−6¢
4¢	3¢

7	6
−2	+3
5	9

Page 113

6¢   30¢   42¢
59, 60, 61, 62
10:30   4:00   2:30
6 centimeters   3 centimeters
2 inches   4 inches

Page 114

4	9	10	8	8
9	10	8	7	9
34	74	46	57	79
2	6	1	1	6
6	3	2	4	5
20	22	35	43	5

Page 115

8	10	9	4	3
78	59	45	70	14
11	14	12	18	16
15	13	13	14	17
6	7	3	6	9
4	7	9	8	9

Page 116

2	9	38¢	47	7	13
+6	−8	−23¢	+31	+9	−7
8	1	15¢	78	16	6

SPECTRUM

All our workbooks meet school curriculum guidelines and correspond to
The McGraw-Hill Companies classroom textbooks.

DOLCH Sight Word Activities

The DOLCH Sight Word Activities workbooks use the classic Dolch list of 220 basic vocabulary words that make up from 50% to 75% of all reading matter that children ordinarily encounter. Since these words are ordinarily recognized on sight, they are called *sight words*. Volume 1 includes 110 sight words. Volume 2 covers the remainder of the list. 160 pages. Answer key included.

TITLE	ISBN	PRICE
Grades K-1 Vol. 1	1-56189-917-8	$9.95
Grades K-1 Vol. 2	1-56189-918-6	$9.95

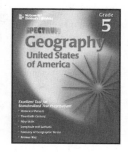

GEOGRAPHY

Full-color, three-part lessons strengthen geography knowledge and map reading skills. Focusing on five geographic themes including location, place, human/environmental interaction, movement, and regions. Over 150 pages. Glossary of geographical terms and answer key included.

TITLE	ISBN	PRICE
Grade 3, Communities	1-56189-963-1	$8.95
Grade 4, Regions	1-56189-964-X	$8.95
Grade 5, USA	1-56189-965-8	$8.95
Grade 6, World	1-56189-966-6	$8.95

MATH

Features easy-to-follow instructions that give students a clear path to success. This series has comprehensive coverage of the basic skills, helping children to master math fundamentals. Over 150 pages. Answer key included.

TITLE	ISBN	PRICE
Grade K	1-56189-900-3	$8.95
Grade 1	1-56189-901-1	$8.95
Grade 2	1-56189-902-X	$8.95
Grade 3	1-56189-903-8	$8.95
Grade 4	1-56189-904-6	$8.95
Grade 5	1-56189-905-4	$8.95
Grade 6	1-56189-906-2	$8.95
Grade 7	1-56189-907-0	$8.95
Grade 8	1-56189-908-9	$8.95

PHONICS/WORD STUDY

Provides everything children need to build multiple skills in language. Focusing on phonics, structural analysis, and dictionary skills, this series also offers creative ideas for using phonics and word study skills in other language areas. Over 200 pages. Answer key included.

TITLE	ISBN	PRICE
Grade K	1-56189-940-2	$8.95
Grade 1	1-56189-941-0	$8.95
Grade 2	1-56189-942-9	$8.95
Grade 3	1-56189-943-7	$8.95
Grade 4	1-56189-944-5	$8.95
Grade 5	1-56189-945-3	$8.95
Grade 6	1-56189-946-1	$8.95

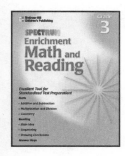

ENRICHMENT MATH AND READING

Books in this series offer advanced math and reading for students excelling in grades 3–6. Lessons follow the same curriculum children are being taught in school while presenting the material in a way that children feel challenged. 160 pages. Answer key included.

TITLE	ISBN	PRICE
Grade 3	1-57768-503-2	$8.95
Grade 4	1-57768-504-0	$8.95
Grade 5	1-57768-505-9	$8.95
Grade 6	1-57768-506-7	$8.95

Prices subject to change without notice.

READING

This full-color series creates an enjoyable reading environment, even for below-average readers. Each book contains captivating content, colorful characters, and compelling illustrations, so children are eager to find out what happens next. Over 150 pages. Answer key included.

TITLE	ISBN	PRICE
Grade K	1-56189-910-0	$8.95
Grade 1	1-56189-911-9	$8.95
Grade 2	1-56189-912-7	$8.95
Grade 3	1-56189-913-5	$8.95
Grade 4	1-56189-914-3	$8.95
Grade 5	1-56189-915-1	$8.95
Grade 6	1-56189-916-X	$8.95

SPELLING

This full-color series links spelling to reading and writing, and increases skills in words and meanings, consonant and vowel spellings, and proofreading practice. Over 200 pages. Speller dictionary and answer key included.

TITLE	ISBN	PRICE
Grade 1	1-56189-921-6	$8.95
Grade 2	1-56189-922-4	$8.95
Grade 3	1-56189-923-2	$8.95
Grade 4	1-56189-924-0	$8.95
Grade 5	1-56189-925-9	$8.95
Grade 6	1-56189-926-7	$8.95

WRITING

Lessons focus on creative and expository writing using clearly stated objectives and pre-writing exercises. Eight essential reading skills are applied. Activities include main idea, sequence, comparison, detail, fact and opinion, cause and effect, making a point, and point of view. Over 130 pages. Answer key included.

TITLE	ISBN	PRICE
Grade 1	1-56189-931-3	$8.95
Grade 2	1-56189-932-1	$8.95
Grade 3	1-56189-933-X	$8.95
Grade 4	1-56189-934-8	$8.95
Grade 5	1-56189-935-6	$8.95
Grade 6	1-56189-936-4	$8.95
Grade 7	1-56189-937-2	$8.95
Grade 8	1-56189-938-0	$8.95

TEST PREP

Prepares children to do their best on current editions of the five major standardized tests. Activities reinforce test-taking skills through examples, tips, practice, and timed exercises. Subjects include reading, math, language arts, writing, social studies, and science. Over 150 pages. Answer key included.

TITLE	ISBN	PRICE
Grades 1-2	1-57768-672-1	$9.95
Grade 3	1-57768-673-X	$9.95
Grade 4	1-57768-674-8	$9.95
Grade 5	1-57768-675-6	$9.95
Grade 6	1-57768-676-4	$9.95
Grade 7	1-57768-677-2	$9.95
Grade 8	1-57768-678-0	$9.95

LANGUAGE ARTS

Encourages creativity and builds confidence by making writing fun! Seventy-two four-part lessons strengthen writing skills by focusing on parts of speech, word usage, sentence structure, punctuation, and proofreading. Each level includes a Writer's Handbook at the end of the book that offers writing tips. This series is based on the highly respected SRA/McGraw-Hill language arts series. More than 180 full-color pages. Answer key included.

TITLE	ISBN	PRICE
Grade 2	1-56189-952-6	$8.95
Grade 3	1-56189-953-4	$8.95
Grade 4	1-56189-954-2	$8.95
Grade 5	1-56189-955-0	$8.95
Grade 6	1-56189-956-9	$8.95

Prices subject to change without notice.

PRESCHOOL

Learning Letters offers comprehensive instruction and practice in following directions, recognizing and writing upper- and lowercase letters, and beginning phonics. Math Readiness features activities that teach such important skills as counting, identifying numbers, creating patterns, and recognizing "same and different." Basic Concepts and Skills offers exercises that help preschoolers identify colors, read and write words, identify simple shapes, and more. 160 pages.

TITLE	ISBN	PRICE
Learning Letters	1-57768-329-3	$8.95
Math Readiness	1-57768-339-0	$8.95
Basic Concepts and Skills	1-57768-349-8	$8.95